DR. RO

COMPOSED

THE HEART AND SCIENCE

OF LEADING

UNDER PRESSURE

dustjacket

Dust Jacket Press
P.O. Box 721243
Oklahoma City, OK 73172
www.dustjacket.com

Ordering information for print editions:
Quantity sales. Special discounts are available on quantity purchases by corporations, associations, and others. For details, contact the Dust Jacket Press address above.

Individual sales. Dust Jacket Press publications are available through most bookstores. They can also be ordered directly from Dust Jacket: Tel: (800) 495-0192; Email: info@dustjacket.com; website: www.dustjacket.com

Dust Jacket logos are registered trademarks of Dust Jacket Press, Inc.

Cover & interior design: D.E. West, ZAQ Designs / Dust Jacket Creative Services

Printed in the United States of America

www.dustjacket.com

TABLE OF CONTENTS:

ACKNOWLEDGEMENTS:

The completion of most major projects takes a village, and this is no exception. There are so many people who have helped me become a more composed version of myself over the years, who supported me and the completion of this book, and who have been my role models.

Special thanks go to Kellie Roberts, my real time editor, for meeting with me every Tuesday for a year to help me get my research and experiences into a book. This project would not have been completed without your patience, finely tuned ear, and conscientiousness, Kellie. Thank you.

And thanks to my other editors along the way including Kaylin Sallenback, Rachel Shannon, Jacob Redding, and Grant Learned for your discerning and wise editing voices and pens. And thanks to Jay Cordova, my kindred freak leader, who has believed in me from the start. Jay, you are a gift.

Thanks to all the rest of you wonderfully weird members of my research team including Robleh Kirce, Kira Wenzel, Diana Ecker, Deanna Haney-Loehlein, Jessica Loving, McKendree Hickory, Amy Nagley, Stepanie Lopez, Kayla Logan, Gabrielle Metzler, JD Landers, Emily Minaker, Annie Barthel, Reetu Sandhu, Megan Furstenberg, Liz Pavese-Kaplan, Caitlin Wasilewski, Terran Mackman, Victoria Campbell-Slosberg, Katrina Boshuizen, Tanya Boyd, Rachel Kirce, and Kayla Lozano. You all have put up with the way I mentor and think for years, and have been the catalysts for deep and insightful thinking on what it means to show up our best under pressure.

My brother Doug McKenna has been such a gift to me as a friend, mentor, and big brother. What a blessing to have a built in coach like you who is one of the world's leading experts on the topic of leading from where we stand. Thanks for your love and encouragement, and belief in me.

Thanks to Paul Yost, Joey Collins, Margaret Diddams, and Dana Kendall, my colleagues at Seattle Pacific University. Paul, your partnership and brotherhood in this work over the years has given me the courage to believe we were onto something. Joey, our work together on helping leaders be more composed and your support is priceless. Margaret, having a sister and colleague who knows my history and heart has meant more than you know. And Dana, you push me to bring rigor right alongside the deeper questions of faith. Thanks team.

David and Janet McKenna, you are my role models of what it means to work hard at leading well every day. Mom and Dad, thank you for that gift. Your strength and character is present in every positive strategy in this book.

Thanks to my family – Jackie, Aidan and Ryan. I am so grateful for the grace you've offered me when I've lost my composure and for your willingness to let me test my working theories on you. I love you three so much.

And finally, thank you, God, for your patience and unending grace. Without that, I wouldn't have known where to begin.

INTRODUCTION:

I often ask people this question: "If you could pick one word that describes what you want to be more like under pressure, what would it be?" The responses include things like patient, connected, clear, calm, resilient, assertive – and composed is almost always near the top of the list. There is something deep inside each of us that desires to be a better version of ourselves when the storms of life hit us, and to be the same in the midst of trials or triumphs that we know are coming, but can't always predict.

My purpose in writing this book is to help you maintain your composure and show up well when the pressure on you is highest – not only for your sake, but for the sake of those around you. Although much of my work has been with leaders, you certainly don't need to have the title "leader" to know that pressure, anxiety, and conflict are realities in life. Whether it is a fear of conflict, public exposure, or a failure related to your family, friends, or work, pressure and anxiety are realities in our daily lives. We all face pressure, and the impact on us and on those around us can be significant.

Wouldn't it be great if all of us could become a little bit better at handling pressure? If in these moments, we could show up better, hold onto ourselves, and maintain our ability to listen and stay connected to others? My hope is that you will see yourself in these pages, identify and embrace practical strategies for better handling pressure, and develop your capacity to be your best self when the stakes are high. I not only want this for you, but for everyone around you and for those who matter most to you.

I am driven by my fundamental belief that we must build up leaders who have a strong sense of themselves, and an equally strong ability to see other people. My intention is not to make you into someone who you are not, but to develop your capacity to step out and be a stronger version of yourself, to maintain your ability to listen to others, to see what matters to them, and to lead well - even when you are scared, anxious, or reluctant. How we show up under pressure is just as important as what we do.

For me, this book is deeply personal and deeply professional. I have seen the impact of my own ability (and inability) to maintain my composure in both my work and family relationships. Whether it's a disagreement with a family member, a conflict at work, or being at the edge of my confidence or comfort zone, my capacity to hold onto myself and stay connected to those around me matters.

Like so many people in my world, I know what it's like to feel the pressure and wish that I could show up differently. In those moments, it always feels like something big is on the line. Although something may or may not be actually changing, it's my feelings about myself, my relationships, or something significant that moves front and center. Times of high pressure produce all kinds of different responses inside of us. Feelings of shame, discouragement about our lack of forward progress, fear of the unknown, and frustration with other people can take over. These are the times when many of us have reached for some piece of advice, a voice of encouragement, and called out to God for wisdom, discernment, and composure necessary to not only feel better, but to behave better for the sake of those around us.

The good news is that we are not alone. Maintaining our composure when it matters most isn't challenging because others don't experience it as a challenge, it's challenging because we haven't given ourselves permission to show up as our vulnerable selves. Vulnerability requires us to open ourselves up to the possibility of being hurt, and that takes a tremendous amount of courage and sacrificial character. So many of us want to become better people and leaders, and desire real and vulnerable conversations about what we experience when the pressure is on us.

THE RESEARCH BEHIND THE BOOK

For fifteen years, we have studied the impact of pressure on leaders and the strategies that allowed them to navigate important moments. Our research is based on responses to several versions of the following questions we have asked people.

1. Think about a recent high-pressure situation that you have faced or are currently facing - one that has challenged your personal convictions and your ability to stay connected to the thoughts, needs, and feelings of other people involved. This situation might include a direct conflict, a conversation you need to have, or a person or group who is challenging for you in some way. What is this situation and why it is challenging for you?

2. What allowed you to stay connected to others involved in this situation, and what allowed you stay true to what mattered to you?

In analyzing all the responses, we've learned a tremendous

amount about the situations that cause pressure for people, the fundamental tension that pressure creates in each of us, and the strategies that allow us to show up well when it matters most. This book highlights all of these things, and hopefully, will create moments where you can look back and say, "I know my tendencies when things get tough, and I've learned how to hang in there for myself and for others."

Our findings are also based on responses to an assessment known as the Leading Under Pressure Inventory, one tool in a set of eight personal development tools designed to prepare leaders who have both a sense of themselves and a connection to the needs of others. For more information on using this tool or others, go to: *www.wildtoolkit.com*

STRUCTURE OF THE BOOK

The book is divided into two main sections. The first three chapters set the stage by describing the daily pressures we face and how they impact us. The remaining chapters describe the eleven strategies we've discovered in our research that allow people to hold onto them-selves and stay connected to others when everything inside of you is telling you to focus on one or the other, or to simply bail out because the pressure is just too high.

These strategies are key ingredients to being more composed when it matters most. While none of us are effective at using all the strategies in this book, we all have strengths that are important for us to see and leverage. Similarly, we all have areas where a little improvement could have a profound impact on us and those around us. If you are interested in investing in becoming a better version of yourself when the pressure is on, for the sake of your own health and for the sake of others around you, then this book is written for you.

CHAPTER 1 | "WELCOME TO THE AMAZING RACE!"

"Pressure is often unavoidable, but how we deal with it is not."

I'll never forget the anxiety I felt the first time I was asked to speak in a church. I was asked by the pastor to play Phil from *The Amazing Race.*[1] Although speaking in front of business people wouldn't have even caused a blip on my anxiety screen, speaking in front of a church was entirely different. Looking back, I now realize that the anxiety came from (1) my perceptions of who was "supposed" to speak in church and (2) my inability to act. Although I knew I was pretty good at speaking from my gut, acting and speaking from a script were new for me. I was also anxious because I grew up in a church where only theologically educated people spoke up front. This all brought me to this moment where I was feeling, "I am not worthy to be on this stage."

1. Doganieri, E., van Munster, B., & Weinstein, E. (Writers), & Doganieri, E., & Weinstein, E. (Directors). (2001). The amazing race [*Television series*]. In J. Bruckheimer, E. Doganieri, B. van Munster, J. Littman, & H. Washington (Producers). United States: Columbia Broadcasting System.

The script was simple and went something like this: "Welcome to the amazing race. This race will take teams to thirty-two countries and six continents all around the globe. Twenty-four contestants will take part in this amazing race around the world!" I correctly said the first sentence. "Welcome to the amazing race!" I then glanced up to see my wife's face in the audience and my mind went blank. Her face was clearly communicating (or so I thought), "Please either get a hold of yourself or make it stop and get off the stage!"

While I now know this wasn't what she was thinking, that's what I thought. To my disappointment, the rest of my acting went from the possibility of being okay to being a disaster of awkward starts and stops. This was one of many ineffective moments in my life where my inability to compose myself was exposed. Even though I don't experience that kind of anxiety when speaking in churches today, I'm not immune to it creeping back into my consciousness in other situations – situations where my negative self-talk and my lack of confidence or actual ability meet in a swirl of ineffectiveness. The perception and the weight we put on outcomes plays into that anxiety. The more important I perceive the outcome to be, the more I'm risking, and the greater my anxiety. This can happen even in a circumstance where I might otherwise have confidence. Whether speaking in a church or having a conversation with someone close where I feel something is at risk, that anxiety can impact my ability to "show up" well.

Composed is the state of standing firmly in who we are while staying connected to those who matter most to us - especially when those unpredictable high pressure moments come. Who among us wouldn't want that? It doesn't matter whether you are a CEO, a parent, a manager for the first time, or a student, high pressure moments challenge all of us. I have worked with enough people to know that none of us are immune to the possibility of losing it when we are under pressure. Different things cause each of us to lose our ability to hold onto ourselves – to be composed. For some people, public speaking is a fear. Maybe conflict makes you uncomfortable. For others, simply being responsible for the experience or learning of others (being the leader) causes you anxiety. Even for seasoned leaders who face pressure every day, showing up their best can be tough. We all face different fears of being exposed and experience situations in which we try to hold onto ourselves and make things better for others. Whether anxiety makes us feel incompetent and unworthy, or mean and reactive, the impact of losing our composure is significant.

Most of us face high pressure situations more often than we would like. In some cases, we have brought these situations on ourselves, and in other cases, they have been the result of circumstances that are outside of our control. You may be facing the need to have a dreaded conversation with someone close to you, or have been asked to speak in front of a group - and that is enough to make you feel sick. You may work with a person who taxes you emotionally, and because you spend so much time managing your relationship, there is little time left to do much else. Or, you may have taken on a leadership role in an area where you don't have much confidence. In these situations and in all the others that tax us emotionally, mentally, and even physically, the common reality is that the stakes feel high.

High pressure moments are both a blessing and a curse. They're blessings because they have the power to teach us something, or to release a possibility that we couldn't see otherwise. They have the power to change our perspective, and to offer a view of a better future for us and for those in our care. At the same time, they feel like tests that we can either pass or fail. The passes have tremendous power, but the failures are just as powerful. The failures haunt us because of the trail of destruction that sometimes results. Broken relationships, failed businesses, shame, doubt, and feelings of letting others down – all results of tests we believe we failed, or actually failed. That's the reality. Pressure is as real as the conflicts, arguments, and changes that cause it to happen inside of us.

Pressure is often unavoidable, but how we deal with it is not. The problem is that we so often blame pressure and anxiety as the causes of the outcomes we see. When we do that, we fail to see that pressure is the catalyst, but not necessarily the uncontrollable circumstance. In some cases, it was our inability to handle it that may have made the difference.

If…we could have been just a little better at handling the storm, we might have been able to play a better part in saving a failing marriage and even making it thrive, to lead our business through a downward swing in the economy, or even to provide calm and clear thinking for others in the midst of a heated argument that would eventually tear a community, a business, a church, or a friendship apart.

These pressured moments are challenging because of both the players and the potential impacts. We are constrained by our own weaknesses, challenged by the weaknesses of others, and anxious about the impact a bad outcome may have. But, because of the impacts on ourselves and those around us, these pressured moments are among the most important moments in our lives. Therefore, it's necessary to understand both the destructive and redemptive possibilities of handling pressure more effectively. Most importantly, if we are willing to sacrifice, to see things differently, to be the first to ask for forgiveness, and to show a different kind of courage, we can take part in creating a different future that is more aligned with the outcomes we seek.

When we feel responsible for other people, we come face-to-face with pressure. Although pressure is challenging, there is an upside. Pressure is an indicator that something is changing, and change introduces the possibility that we'll learn something new. I'm not talking about simply learning a new skill, but the possibility that we'll fundamentally change who we are and how we show up. While the core DNA of our character isn't likely to change, we are constantly molded and shaped by our environment and by the positive and negative experiences we encounter.

You might be thinking to yourself, "Great, so you're telling me that pressure creates the opportunity to become better at leading other people?" To which I would say, yes, that's exactly right. The high pressure moments we face are oftentimes moments we wouldn't choose. These moments feel like tests that challenge our identity, our relationships, and our feelings about ourselves. Nonetheless, it's clear from our research and conversations with thousands of people that these are the moments offering us the deepest insights. We may not need to throw ourselves into these situations all the time, but simply reframe how we think about them. Like iron being formed in the fire, situations we describe as high pressure provide the heat necessary to build our character, to rely on others, and to learn new things about ourselves, our world, and others around us.

Pressure brings us face-to-face with the possibility that things could be different. You might discover you have a God-given gift that you didn't know you had, or strengths you didn't realize could be developed. It's a matter of becoming aware of when the pressure is on you, identifying your habits that may be getting in the way of remaining composed, and getting intentional about doing something differently. My hope for you is that you'll become aware of those moments when you're feeling pressure, you will reframe them, and will see them as a possibility to learn something. As a result, you might become a better leader, friend, family member, and version of yourself.

THAT PRESSURE FEELING

Many people don't enjoy flying. The dreaded security lines, lack of legroom, crying babies, and lost baggage all contribute to it. However, for some travelers, the greatest issue is the ear pain that happens when the cabin pressure increases. Think about the last time you sat on an airplane as it was ascending and you felt your ears fill up with pressure. The reason you know there is a change is because your ears are popping. Without that feeling, you wouldn't realize that anything was changing. You can't see the pressure, but you know it's there.

In a similar way, we all face situations, conflicts, and conversations that are like that ear pain. Pressure is our internal gauge that tells us that something important may be happening. We can't see it, but we know it when it happens. Something as simple as that email from your boss or a phone call from a troubled family member may cause it for you.

Think about a high pressure situation you faced in the last week. Was it a moment where you felt pressure inside of yourself, but no one else around you felt anything? Did it involve a direct or potential conflict with someone else? Or, was the pressure caused by something that changed in your environment? You may feel that your situation had all three going on at the same time. In what ways was that situation triggered by something inside of you? In what ways was it triggered by your relationship to someone else? Or, was it triggered by something around you that may have been outside of your control?

The table below describes the different kinds of pressures we face and their impact on what we think, how we feel about ourselves and others, and what actions we'll take to deal with the pressure. The point is that pressure sometimes occurs inside of us, between us and others around us, and sometimes simply because something is changing in our environment that we can't control.

		Potential Impact of Pressure		
		Thinking (Cognitive)	Feeling (Emotional)	Doing (Behavioral)
Faces of Pressure	Inside You (Intrapersonal)	Thinking about yourself, and not them	Feeling insecure	Hiding or Boasting
	You and Them (Interpersonal)	Thinking about what others think of you	Feeling like it's a fight	Peacekeeping or Conquering
	Around You (Enviromental)	Thinking about limitations	Feeling overwhelmed	Quitting or Compulsive Action

When we experience pressure that may or may not actually involve others (intrapersonal), it oftentimes causes us to ruminate about ourselves and miss the needs of others, highlights our insecurities, and may cause us to hide behind those emotions. That hiding may be perceived by others as either introversion or arrogance. In either case, it's a way to disguise the impact of the pressure on us.

When the pressure involves our relationship with others (interpersonal), we likely think about others, but mostly what they think about us. This produces emotions and reactions that either cause us to attempt to make everyone feel better, or to conquer the people and the situation. The challenge is that it feels like a fight – a moment to stand up for ourselves and to win.

The final possibility is that the pressure may be caused by something in our environment that is completely outside of our control. Changes in the economy, a couple you know going through a divorce, or someone else at work losing their job – these are moments where we're tempted to focus on scarcity and limitations (what we don't have). Whether it's a scarcity of confidence, trust, or actual physical resources, we feel a limitation that may overwhelm us when we don't know how to respond.

While it would be easier to deal with one piece at a time, the reality is that the intrapersonal, interpersonal, and environmental pressures around us are related. What's happening between us and others is impacting our beliefs about who we are, and our perceptions of the situations happening around us. Likewise, our feelings about ourselves constantly impact how we interact with others and our environment. If you don't believe me, ask any therapist who has seen hundreds of individuals and couples attempting to make sense out of the conflicts and tensions in their lives. If you're like me, trying to understand the relationship between all of these things is not only tiring, but seems really time consuming. The first step is to simply acknowledge that what you believe about yourself, how you relate to others, and what's going around you are in a constant dance with one another.

FOR EXAMPLE…

Imagine a situation in which a colleague of yours is laid off. While you may feel that you were doing a good job at work right up to that moment, this situation causes you to question whether or not you are next to get that notice from your manager. That possibility may then impact the next conversation you have with your manager. Or, imagine that a friend of yours confesses to having had an affair. If you are married, the subsequent conversations with your spouse may start with your friend's marriage and the pain they are feeling, but it's possible that they may lead to questions about the integrity of your own relationship.

Here's the deal – pressure is a reality, but how you respond is a choice. You can build a wall around yourself to avoid pressure, or you can try to medicate it or suppress it. Regardless, you will face pressure. Pressure is an indicator that something is changing and how you respond or learn from the pressure could change your life and relationships. Pressure impacts how we think and feel about ourselves, our relationships, and the things happening around us. It's not something you can see or touch, but it's an invisible force set off by indicators inside of you. If we begin to see pressure for what it is, and make choices about how we are going to think, feel, and act when it comes, what would be the impact on us and on the other important people in our lives? Understanding the impact of pressure is the start, and imagining the possibility of a different response is the first step.

GETTING PERSONAL ABOUT PRESSURE:

1. What is the most recent experience you've had where you've felt your pressure indicator go off (e.g., someone disagreed with you, someone expected you to change, or the circumstances of your life felt out of control)?

2. How do you physically experience pressure? Does your heart race? Does your face become flushed? Do you

sweat? Do you tap your foot? Do you talk too much? Do you become very quiet?

3. In what ways do you experience internal, interpersonal, and environmental pressure?

4. If you could be the person that others need you be under pressure, what would you be like?

CHAPTER 2 | THE FOUNDATION

"We are only victims of the high pressure moments if we choose to be."

Have you ever considered buying a boat? Several years ago, I went from considering it to actually doing it. I wanted a boat for a while and finally convinced my wife that buying a boat would be a great decision for us. I had it all worked out. We had the space to store it and the money saved up. I wasn't naïve enough to think that this boat ownership effort was going to be a walk in the park, but I also didn't know just how far outside the park it was going to take me in the coming weeks.

Have you ever had a moment when something you've long thought about comes face to face with the reality that you're about to actually do that thing? On the drive home from picking up the boat, it hit me. For the first time, I came face to face with the reality that the boat launch near my house was the most narrow and heavily trafficked boat launch I've ever seen.

The first sunny day came about two days later, and my wife suggested that we take the boat out. "Of course!" I responded. "Yes, let's go!" What she didn't know was that my nerves were already starting to get the best of me. We packed up the boat, loaded our four and six-year-old boys into the back of the truck, and picked up my dad on the way to that dreaded boat launch on the shore of Lake Washington. When we arrived, a little old man was pulling his small fishing boat out of the lake. I was relieved to see he was the only one there. Once he was done, I could practice my boat backing skills with only my family members as witnesses. Then it happened. My idealized plan ran into a real world problem. That little old man took about 30 minutes to pull his boat out of the water, and by the time he was done, there were eight or nine trucks lined up behind me. Whether or not they knew what they were doing wasn't important to me. Their trucks and boats looked much more impressive than mine, and I felt the pressure rising.

At that point, my kids and my wife got out of the truck and my dad went to the back of the boat to give me hand signals. I had rules in my head about which way to turn the steering wheel when looking out the back window. (Oh, by the way, an important piece of information that I left out of my story is that I've never backed up a boat trailer in my life. That will be important later). When it came to backing up boat trailers, my dad had a different set of rules in his head. He believed that making certain circular hand motions would tell me which way to turn the steering wheel. I knew my rules worked, but I also knew that his rules worked for him. As if backing the boat into the launch wasn't challenging enough, there was also a timed post that would raise and lower after swiping a key card over a sensor. I had a minute or so to get the boat trailer over the post before it would go back up again.

So imagine this silly moment and the multiple voices in my head. I know my steering wheel rules; I'm aware that my kids and my wife are ready to be boating; I know my dad has his own set of rules; I realize that there are many competent boaters waiting to put their boats in the water, and I'm also aware that there is a stupid post that has this whole process on a timer.

It took me over a dozen stressful starts and stops to get the boat into the water. As I sat there with the trailer, I felt a sense of relief. What I didn't realize was that it wasn't quite over. When I put the truck into drive to pull the trailer out of the water, I heard a woman scream, "Jesus Christ!" After I realized she wasn't praying for me, I slammed on the brakes, realizing that my passenger door was wide open and was about to slam into a metal pole. I closed the door and pulled the truck out of the way for my new friends with their impressive trucks and boats. I put my truck in park and just sat there. In that moment I thought to myself, "I never want to feel this way again."

You probably understand that my stress wasn't just about the boat and my lack of experience backing boat trailers. This experience was a collision of voices in my head that involved my perceptions and the realities related to my competence, the people that surrounded me, the structures that had been built long before I arrived at the boat launch, and my feelings about myself all coming together in a mess of ridiculousness. Although on the surface this may seem like an overstatement, the reality is that every high pressure situation, and our ability to cope with them, occurs on top of a foundation of things that are oftentimes invisible to us when we are right in the moment. My boat story may be a silly example, but an example nonetheless of what everyday pressure feels like when our knowledge and competence come into contact with the needs of others around us. Whether you're backing a boat, or responding to a reactive email from a coworker, many of the causes of pressure are rooted in that chemical mix of competence, community, culture, and character.

The remainder of this book will be about your habits under pressure, and strengths you can build on to remain composed when it matters most, understanding our strengths, the people that surround us, the rules of engagement, and our basic make-up.

PREPARING FOR PRESSURE

Just because you walked across the stage at your high school graduation doesn't mean you were prepared for college. Hopefully graduating was an indication of that preparation, but there was likely an important list of other fundamentals that were going to be the keys to your success at the next level. Factors that prepared you for what came next hopefully had been in place long before you started applying to different colleges or jobs – a foundation of basic writing and communication skills, a family or community that supports you, and an educational system that challenged you and built your character.

If you've ever played amateur contractor for a project at your house that involved structural changes, you've experienced the necessity for a foundation. Ten years ago, contractors replaced a pair of posts that held up our patio roof. Because we are now replacing the patio, I have discovered that those contractors failed to set those posts on a foundation of concrete, but instead simply put the posts in the ground. Ten years later, they are once again rotten and will need to be replaced. I didn't know better back then, but I know better this time around.

In the same way, there are fundamentals that, if we can get them in place, will provide the necessary foundation for handling life's pressures more effectively. It isn't enough to just put posts in place. It's necessary to build our actions around a foundation that's as solid as we can make it.

COMPETENCE

Most high pressure situations we face not only require some sort of actual skill, but involve our confidence in our ability to do that skill. Have you ever experienced someone who, in a moment of weakened inhibition, started to sing along with the radio? You realize that this person has a beautiful voice and so you tell them, "You have a beautiful singing voice." What sometimes follows your compliment is, "No, no, no, I can't sing." In psychological terms, that belief in our ability is called self-efficacy. Our actual skills and our beliefs about those skills have a profound impact on how we show up under pressure.

I believe that most people would perceive me as a fairly confident and self-assured person. I'm not saying it because I always feel it, but because others have told me so. It often surprises me because, like many people, I am very aware of my insecurities and levels of actual and perceived incompetence. Nothing has illustrated the power of confidence related to my ability to be composed more than my time as a musician. When you are on a stage rehearsing with gifted musicians, nothing will reduce you to a useless bowl of mush more than when you are asked to play a guitar solo for which you haven't prepared. I am a decent guitar player; however, I never devoted enough time refining my skills to be able to improvise on the spot. This is why rehearsal, feedback, and courage can all help to prepare us for these moments.

If you don't have the time to prepare, be cautious of overstating your lack of preparation as a lack of the ability to learn a particular skill. At an even deeper level, some of us have a tendency to let our perceptions of our competence creep into our identity and our deeper feelings about ourselves. Our perceptions around our lack of ability could be based on something that simply isn't true. I'm not suggesting we're all good singers, but that we need to be thoughtful in labeling our inability to be competent in a high pressure moment as a general lack of competence. Given time and dedication, almost anyone can learn to be more competent in high pressure situations.

COMMUNITY

Another important foundation you can build to set yourself up to be more composed under pressure is the community of people that surround you. Similar to competence, community not only includes those actual people, but the extent to which we believe that they are there to support us. In my research team's investment in hundreds of leaders, we have encouraged each leader to consider the strategic network of people surrounding them. This network includes the people who give them feedback, supports them when they take risks, and helps them identify possibilities in the face of situations where they may not see a way out.

Without that community, high pressure situations can become overwhelming and even paralyzing. We oftentimes dismiss these kinds of relationships as either touchy-feely or overly mechanized when they are labeled strategic. However, it is these relationships that often provide a buffer against all the voices in our heads that tell us lies about us being under-qualified, unworthy, or less than we really are. Hopefully you've experienced this before. It's a lot easier to make a leap of faith when you know there are some people around you who will love you whether you succeed or fail, that will encourage you to take a risk, and give you advice on what to do after you jump, and what you might feel when you do. If identifying that that network of support seems overwhelming to you, you aren't alone.

When we coach leaders, whether they are parents or presidents, establishing a list of the people who play strategic support roles in their lives always requires vulnerability and courage. That feeling of uncertainty about who supports you is a common feeling. The power is moving through that feeling and getting on with establishing that community of support. There are people all around you who would be willing to support you if you ask.

CULTURE

Culture surrounds all of us. Culture is an invisible force that tells us what's appropriate, what rules to follow, and what's most important. Think about a specific area of your life where you feel some responsibility.

1. What are the stated or unstated rules of engagement in that area of your life?

2. What's the first thing that comes to mind when you think about those rules of engagement?

Culture is impacted by physical objects and rules that we've experienced for so long that we no longer notice them. Similar to a light turning red at an intersection we drive through every day that causes us to stop, that invisible culture has the power to impact everything we do. Whether they are physical objects or assumptions we follow on auto-pilot, culture includes things that are difficult for us to identify, but not difficult for us to follow. When we're in high pressure situations, we enter into working principles and rules that we've internalized. These are things that not only impact how we behave, but influence how we feel about ourselves.

For the past two decades, I've reminded students that when they enter the working world, there will be an invisible culture that could begin to define them. Without being aware of it, they may become slaves to cultural pressures. While that sounds dark and dreary, there is an upside. Mindfulness about the culture that surrounds us can provide the necessary launching pad for us to become the better versions of ourselves when the stakes are high.

Returning to my boat story, I now realize that the boat launch I described is ridiculously narrow compared to most other launches. Not only that, it also happens to be situated in the middle of town, making it a prime spectator sport for passersby hanging out on the dock. If I'd understood the basic culture I was a part of that day, things might have gone differently. I might have practiced more frequently in a situation or place where I wasn't going to be exposed, or I might have chosen to drive an extra fifteen minutes to another boat launch. Being aware of that may have made all the difference in the world that first time.

CHARACTER

Character is something we all have. At the most fundamental level, character is an imprint. It's the culmination of all the relationships and moments of our lives. Like a Douglas fir growing out of a cliff that overlooks the ocean, our character has been shaped by the winds that have blown in our faces for years, by the water that has fed our roots, and by the people who have carved their names in the bark that has served to protect us.

What we oftentimes miss is the power of our choices in shaping our character, and it just so happens that moments of high pressure force these choices. These include the choices that impact what we'll do next, who we'll follow, and what we'll believe about ourselves. The choice regarding our character is simple. Will we be willing to become a better version of ourselves for the sake of those around us, or will we lock down and fail to learn in these moments? The type of character we'll embrace makes the difference between us being at the mercy of the storms, or being active participants and leaders through them. We are only victims of the high pressure moments if we choose to be. The pressure can force us to freeze, blame, retreat into ourselves, or it will give us an opportunity to embrace the moment as a moment that matters – a moment to realize there is something to learn that could serve others through our response. It's not easy, especially when we are weary and tired from all the pressure, but it can be powerful if when we realize the opportunity that pressure creates to refine our character.

KNOWING IT WHEN WE FEEL IT

I've talked to enough people to know that we all face moments where pressure gets the best of us. Our research suggests that whether you are a stay-at-home parent or a president, we all face situations that seem normal to others, but personally challenge our capacity to simultaneously stay true to what we know, to listen to others, and to manage the multiple voices in our heads. The good news is that we can build a more solid foundation.

We start by being aware of the places where we feel competent, of the culture that surrounds us, the people that both support and challenge us, and by being willing to change and become better versions of ourselves.

My experience at the boat launch that day was one of a thousand situations I've faced that challenged my capacity to stay composed, to stay true to what I know, and to hear the needs of others. If you're anything like me, the examples come daily. In those moments when we are thinking, "I never want to feel this way again", we have choices to make, even when we feel like we don't. Our first choice is to simply recognize the situations that cause pressure for us, and then to recognize the reality that pressure is often caused by the fundamental tension we feel when our convictions and motivations come face-to-face with the convictions and motivations of others.

BUILDING YOUR FOUNDATION:

1. Think about a high pressure situation that caused you to question your competence. To what extent was your perception of your competence based on your ability to do what you were being asked to do, your perceptions of your ability to do it, the amount of practice time you had put in, or real incompetence that you couldn't learn no matter how hard you tried?

2. On a scale from 1 to 10 (10 is to a higher extent), to what extent are you surrounded by a community of people who both support and challenge you?

3. To what extent are the rules of engagement (whether they are real rules or rules you perceive) impacting how

you show up in that high pressure situation you described in questions 1?

4. To what extent are you willing to change and admit that you're getting it wrong, especially if changing might help others?

CHAPTER 3 | **YOU AND ME:
THE FUNDAMENTAL
TENSION**

*"Whether you spend most of your energy
focusing on pleasing others or most of
your energy on staying true to yourself,
the outcome is the same - self-
preservation."*

When I first started leading workshops focused on helping people be more composed, I would try little tricks to safely increase the pressure on the audience. One of my favorite tricks was telling the audience that I had pre-selected three of them to come up to the front of the room and do something. Depending on the group, I would vary the details of the assignment. In some cases, I'd tell the audience that three of them were going to come up front and describe why they were the most competent person to do their job. With other groups, I would simply tell them that they were going to come up and talk about their strengths.

After making sure they understood what three of them were going to be asked to do, I'd ask them a series of questions. Keep in mind they still didn't know which three people in the room were going to be picked. I first asked them what they were thinking about as they thought about the possibility of being chosen to come up front. People commonly said things like, "I'm thinking about what competence means," "I'm thinking about what I'm good at doing," or "I'm thinking about how my skills match up with my job." Sometimes the response would be, "why are you doing this?" I then asked about what they were feeling at that moment. So often, I heard responses like nervous, anxious, exposed, scared, or overwhelmed. I also heard some positive things like excited and ready.

Whenever I do this exercise, there are always at least two kinds of people in the room. First, there are those who care deeply about what other people think and are focused on those relationships. For many of them, it always feels as if they are under a spotlight and everyone is staring at them. In some cases, this fear of being selected is so great that they forgot what the assignment was in the first place. The second is different. They're focused on the task without giving much thought to how others perceive them. After hearing what the assignment is, many of these individuals think, "I was ready to do this long before this assignment. Give me the mic, McKenna, I'll tell you what I'm good at." I know they think this because they've told me.

The challenge between these two groups is that they don't communicate well. The first group tries to manage relationships and will spend most of their emotional energy trying to maintain the peace, especially when it comes to how people feel about them. The second group will mobilize primarily around the task and what needs to be done, with little consideration for what other people think or feel.

After the audience processes their thoughts and feelings, I tell them my little secret. No one was actually going to come speak up front. My point in introducing the possibility was that in order to fully understand the impact of pressure, I had to find a safe way to introduce an environment likely to highlight their tendencies when something real was on the line.

PEACE-KEEPERS
AND TRUTH-SPEAKERS

In our conversations and research with leaders, we discovered a fundamental tension that a majority of people face when they feel pressure. This tension is often experienced as a conversation going on inside their heads between what they think and what they perceive others to be thinking. You probably experienced this tension today. It may have been a conversation with your spouse, with your roommate, or an email from a co-worker. For some reason, that interaction set off your pressure indicators, and the conversation inside your head began.

Peace-keepers are likable people when the pressure is low. However, the problem with peace-keepers is that pressure will cause them to miss out on a more realistic view of the truth. Peace-keepers, at their worst, will sacrifice everything else to make everyone happy with them. Here's the problem: You can't make everyone happy without lying to someone. The challenge for peace-keepers is to be direct with people. Instead of talking directly with people, they're more likely to talk with others about those people. It's called gossip. We've all experienced this. It's playground behavior. If we don't like what someone is doing, it is sometimes easier to talk about them rather than talk to them directly.

Truth-speakers, on the other hand, are attractive because they give it to us straight. The problem with truth-speakers is that they're only functioning with their version of the story. They don't know what they don't know because they stop asking other people to fill in the blanks. Here's what happens. Even in situations where truth-speakers express openness to feedback, their behavior will tell you that they're actually not open. How many times have we heard a leader say, "I have an open door policy. If you have a problem with me, come and talk with me." Saying something like this doesn't make people do what you've told them to do. The challenge for truth-speakers is realizing that leading well is not only being direct, but also being open to new ways of listening.

Here's another way to think about it. People who have a tendency to speak the truth face a fundamental challenge of being open to the perspective of others. People who make peace face a fundamental challenge of telling people what they think, spending all their energy making sure people are happy with them.

Although we have different tendencies when the pressure is on, there's one thing we all have in common. Pressure has a way of making us more selfish. Whether you spend most of your energy focusing on pleasing others (peace-keepers) or most of your energy on staying true to yourself (truth-speakers), the outcome is the same - self-preservation. We're willing to sacrifice the truth or even our relationships to make sure we feel better. Feeling better may involve making sure we feel like everyone likes us, or that we got our way, but in both cases, it's about us feeling better. From a practical perspective, either tendency can have positive implications for others, as well as a downside.

In a completely objective world, we'd be in a constant and healthy balance between listening to others and listening to our

inner voice. In the real world, it's just not like that. For leaders, being composed is even more complex. It's not just one other voice
they're trying to listen to, but multiple voices for whom they are
responsible, and all who want something different.

If you've ever coached your child's sports team, you know that
every parent on that team has a different opinion. If you've ever
led a small group in your community, church, or child's school, you
know the pressure to lead well and to keep everyone happy with
the group. If you've been an executive, you know the challenge of
maintaining your convictions while listening to the needs of your
board members, employees, leadership team, and customers. If
you've ever had to deal with a difficult person at work or have had
to face a difference of opinion with one of your parents, you know
that the greatest challenge is trying to stay connected to someone with whom you may never agree. The common factor in all of
these examples is that pressure highlights the tension between
you and them.

BUILDING A CULTURE
OF COMPOSURE

Pressure can turn on our ugliness like nothing else. However,
there is another possibility. We could become better equipped
to face the high pressure moments of our lives, and see the perspective of others more effectively, while also staying true to our
own perspective. It may involve working a little harder at how you
show up in high pressure situations and doing something that
feels like a bit of a risk, but it could make all the difference for
yourself or for the people in your world. Our ability to compose
ourselves isn't something we do on our own. It's our combined
strengths that offer the possibility of a very different reality –

a culture within our families, our workplaces, and our communities where composure is the common story and not the exception.

GETTING PERSONAL
ABOUT YOU AND ME:

1. Read the following six pairs of statements comparing statement 1 on the left to statement 2 on the right. In each case, circle the one that best describes you in high pressure situations.

STATEMENT 1	STATEMENT 2
I express my thoughts and feelings without concern for how others will respond.	I am cautious of the way I behave and of what I say to others.
I do what I think is right, regardless of how other people feel about it.	The thoughts and feelings of others impact what I do.
When I am in conflict with another person, it is important for me to express my true feelings.	When I am in conflict with another person, it is important for us to find common ground.
I don't place importance on what others think of me.	I like others to respect me.
I am not concerned about the impression I create with others.	I care about the impression I create with others.
I trust what my gut is telling me when things get tough.	I trust the feedback I receive from others when things get tough.

Count how many statements you circled in the left column. Identify the corresponding number on the left side of the diagram below (i.e, truth-speaker) and trace the circle. Count how many statements you circled in the right column. Identify the corresponding number on the right side of the diagram below (i.e., peace-keeper) and trace the circle. The resulting picture depicts your pressure tendency.

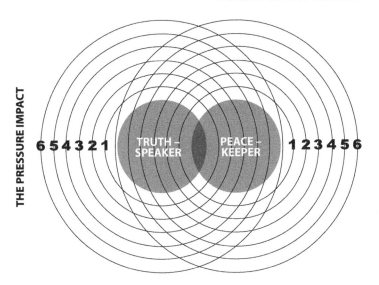

2. If you scored higher as a peace-keeper, what does it feel like to imagine yourself being more direct with others? If you scored higher as a truth-speaker, what does it feel like to imagine spending more time listening to others than telling them what you think?

CHAPTER 4 | ON A MISSION OR ADRIFT: SENSE OF PURPOSE

"Purposeful intention in the back of your mind can serve as the personal keel that will steady you when you hit that next storm."

As children, we naturally ask a lot of questions. When they were younger, my sons were notorious for the "why" questions. "Hey dad, why are spots in a parking lot called stalls?" Why is red the color for stop? Why do the prices of gas go up and down? "Why?" is a difficult question. I can't tell you how many times my response to my sons' questions was, "That's a good question. We should look that up when we get home." When someone else has already answered the question for me, I often don't think about it.

As my boys became older and began to confront the realities of the world, their questions became even more difficult. These questions involved the invisible intentions of others and were rooted in things that are far beyond my understanding or my ability to search the internet for an answer. The other day, my son asked me, "Why would someone break into another person's home? If I did that, I couldn't live with myself." He's also asked, "Why would someone kill children?" These might seem a bit extreme, but these are the questions of "why" that my boys ask.

The stakes become higher when the answers to questions of "why" become intimately connected with our own identity, with the relationships that matter most to us, or things that may be outside of our control. Similar to my son's question about the color of stoplights, it's sometimes easier to respond with, "that's just the way it is," as opposed to uncovering the deeper story of why you're feeling pressure within yourself, between yourself and another person, or within your environment. Are these difficult things that are happening to me happening because of something I did or did not do? Why is that person angry with me? Did I lose my job because I am incompetent or because my organization doesn't appreciate me? Why do good things happen to bad people? Why do bad things happen to good people? Questions of why often cause us to question our own purpose, and sometimes even our value.

When my students are accepted into our graduate program, I talk with them about what I describe as the "imposter syndrome"- that feeling that you have no business being a part of something because you feel drastically underqualified. When they look around and see the caliber of people with whom they have been included, they often become immediately aware of their imposter. It isn't until later that the purpose behind their selection into the program becomes clear, and they see that it's precisely because of that humble awareness of their imposter that we wanted them in the program.

Questions that start with "Why" become even more difficult when they go beyond the imposter syndrome and we're confronted with our own limitations. Why was I not chosen? Why didn't I get any credit? Why are you blaming me? It goes beyond feeling under-qualified to feeling that we may be at fault – even when we may or may not be part of the reason for the result.

PURPOSE THAT HAUNTS ME

We ask "why" all the time, but it's often after something happens around us or to us that we don't fully understand. The fact that we're asking the question in the first place is a reminder that we believe everything should happen for a purpose. When we can't find an answer, purpose can become this haunting question where the answer to "why" is completely unknown. We become aware that important moments in our lives may happen for a reason, or they may be simple happenings – moments that either will never have significance or may have significance in the future.

PURPOSE THAT FINDS ME

It's natural to ask "why" or try to make sense of a situation after the fact. This morning when I got into my office, I realized that I forgot my laptop at home (I happen to have a lot of work to do today with my laptop!). I'm open to the possibility that I forgot my laptop for no reason at all or that the purpose of my forgetfulness will emerge later in my day or week. Although the purpose of my missing laptop may be something beautiful and I'll look back on my day with gratitude, I might be able to take some control back and repurpose my day. Because I can't fight through two hours of traffic to go and get my laptop, what else could I do with this opportunity? What more important and significant purpose could my computer-less day serve? Purpose isn't necessarily something that happens to us or finds us. Purpose can also direct us forward.

PURPOSE THAT DRIVES ME

Our research on strategies that allow people to remain composed under pressure strongly suggests that a person's sense of purpose may be one of the most important trump cards in allowing them to show up best when it matters most. In order for us to clearly identify our purpose, we have to become private detectives into our own lives. We have to be willing to examine the structures around us causing us to feel the way we feel and respond to others in a certain way.

Your purpose is often shaped by your strengths and past experiences, providing you a path forward that is partly directed by your life up to this point. Purpose is also directly tied to your intentions and to what you really want. Stated differently, your purpose is defined by who you are, what you're capable of doing, and what you intend to accomplish. Your capacity to understand why you are struggling to remain composed is directly related to your willingness to define your purpose.

How often have you entered into a high pressure situation or conversation without understanding your purpose for being there? Although it might be okay to begin a road trip without a plan, it's a big risk to head into a high stakes situation or conflict without understanding why you're there in the first place. We all do this at different times, risking the possibility that we'll be derailed by our own anxiety, limitations, and reactivity.

Your sense of purpose and intentionality are powerful things. It's no wonder when we teach people how to ride motorcycles, we tell them, "Look where you want to go, because you'll go where you look." Some of us want to deny the power of intentions and move straight to action. Without understanding our intent for the journey, we inadvertently identify a journey without a destination. Although that certainly might be appropriate at times, when the stakes are high and conflicts are growing, do we really want to risk that our reactivity will take over and our purpose will be lost?

I've seen the power of intent help people, and the lack of it do tremendous damage. If we're going to build up a powerful generation of leaders who have the capacity to confront pressure head on - whether those are conversations with a close friend, or situations where we are confronting injustice in the world - we need to be mindful of the power of purpose and intention. If you're someone who is overwhelmed by the need for others to be pleased with you, purpose can make all the difference in the world. However, it takes a little preplanning before those high pressure moments arrive. Spending 5 minutes at the beginning of the day looking at your calendar of meetings or appointments can make all the difference. For each meeting, consider your purpose for being in that meeting. If you're someone who thinks this is a waste of time, this may work especially well for you. You may believe that thinking about why you're having a conversation with your son's teacher has nothing to do with the actual meeting, but it does. Thinking about your intentions provides the reason you're there and impacts the way you might respond when the meeting gets a little hairy. If you remind yourself that your reason for being there is to improve the experience of your son and the teacher, it can change everything. When your buttons get pushed, purposeful intention in the back of your mind can serve as the personal keel that will steady you when you hit that next storm.

Whether it's a job interview, a conflict at work, or that meeting with your child's teacher, writing down your purpose for being there in the first place is the key.

<u>GETTING ON PURPOSE:</u>

1. If you woke up tomorrow and you were doing exactly what you were supposed to be doing, regardless of the expectations of others, what would you be doing?

2. If you feel like you are off track or simply not doing the work or living the life you want to, what risks are you avoiding taking? Why?

3. If the idea of an overarching purpose is intimidating, consider your purpose today. The meetings you have scheduled today or the moments you have alone all have the potential to be your purpose. If you took the risk to believe that you are in those moments for a reason that creates a positive impact for yourself and for others, what would that purpose be?

4. Think about a high pressure moment you're currently facing. What is your purpose for being in this conversation or situation? What do you hope to maintain or to let go? What do other people need from you?

CHAPTER 5 | # BARRIERS OR POSSIBILITIES: FOCUSING ON POTENTIAL

"One of the most important ways to maintain your composure is to see what could be, despite everything inside of you telling you that things are getting worse."

There's a photo I often refer to with leaders when discussing the development of a mindset focused on potential. The photo shows a large tree that has fallen across a winding road through the woods. If you saw the picture right now, you'd likely see the first thing that I saw, a very large barrier blocking the road. I once asked my two sons to look at this picture and describe the first thing that they noticed. I fully expected it would be a large tree blocking the road. To my surprise, my six year old son said, "Dad, that's cool! I can take a board, run it up that tree, and jump my bike off it!" My eight-year-old son said, "We could cut up that tree and use it for firewood when we camp." My younger son then chimed in again and said, "I see that the road continues beyond the tree."

Why do we start by seeing a tree blocking the road? Perhaps the reality is that children see something that we don't. Maybe there's something about the bumps and bruises we've experienced when facing challenges that have led us to focus on the barriers. Oftentimes, it's the pressure we feel that not only causes us to see the tree as a barrier, but also causes our minds to make those barriers bigger than they actually are.

ENTREPRENEURIAL THINKING

A woman I met several years ago, Dr. Saras Saras-vathy,[2] has spent much of her career studying entrepreneurs. She describes two very different ways of thinking about getting something done. The first way of thinking is what has been commonly taught in American business schools for the past couple decades. It's what Dr. Sarasvathy describes a focus on causation, which involves predetermined goals and gathering the necessary resources to achieve them. She contrasts this with her study of entrepreneurs, whose thinking she describes as focusing on effectuation. Entrepreneurs start with a different set of questions. Who am I? Who do I know? What resources do I have at my fingertips? What can I do with this information? The fundamental difference between causal reasoning and effectual reasoning is whether you start with the destination or with what you already have. If you drop a tree in the path of an entrepreneur, he or she has probably already identified nine other paths that will get them to their destination. This is not to suggest that there isn't a necessity for both types of thinkers. The point is, challenges and barriers that you see may be very real and need to be faced, but there's a very real danger in stopping there. If our only goal is to travel down that road, then what we see is a tree blocking the road. If our thoughts

---

2. Sarasvathy, S. D. (2001). What makes entrepreneurs entrepreneurial? *Darden Business Publishing*, 1-9.

about the road ahead are expanded, the obstacles in front of us are no longer only obstacles, but opportunities to do something different or better.

It's very tempting to spiral into hopelessness and resentment rather than cultivate a mindset that says, "This will not only get better, but I can see exactly how I will make this better." Our capacity to focus on potential when the pressure rises not only opens up solutions, but also is one of the most important strategies for helping us to maintain our composure when it's most challenging to do so.

NOTICING THE HORIZON

When was the last time you remember having a really bad day and at the end of it, you walked out of your office or house and saw a heart-stopping sunset on the horizon? Sunsets remind us that tomorrow is going to bring a new set of possibilities, and that although today was rough, tomorrow offers something very different.

Pressure creates the possibility that we'll focus our attention on the glass being half empty or even half full, missing the multiple possibilities within our reach. A pessimist sees the glass as half empty and an optimist sees the glass as half full. A person focused on potential however, would say to themselves, "I have a half-full glass of water, what can I do with it?" Whether you're a leader in your family, in a business, in a church, or in your community, your ability to see possibilities when others might not opens up new purposes. Maintaining your ability to focus on the potential when the pressure is the highest will help you to hold onto yourself and maintain your composure.

Our challenge is to not only become aware of the moments when we see barriers and lose sight of possibilities, but to understand the impact on ourselves and others, and to take actions that will help us hold the barriers in perspective. Wherever you lead or show up, one of the most important ways to maintain your composure is to see what could be, despite everything inside of you telling you that things are getting worse.

People who focus on potential inspire others to think about possibilities they may not see if that person wasn't in the room. They're not trying to make people happy or to avoid the hard questions. To the contrary, they're oftentimes thinking strategically and in real time about providing more options instead of less. If you could become better at seeing possibilities and potential in situations when the pressure is on, what would be the benefit for you and for those who matter most to you?

People who develop their capacity to focus on potential, engage in what I describe as "this and that" thinking versus "either-or" thinking. Either-or thinkers tend to see one of two options, a good option and a bad option. Developing our capacity to be "this and that" thinkers allows us to see that in every situation, we are presented with multiple paradoxes. This is the reality that what "could be" lives in constant tension with the reality that there are very real barriers in our way at the same time. In many cases, there are multiple possibilities, many of which may have aspects that are both good and bad. Trees crossing roads are both barriers in one sense, and bike jumps in others.

The ability to focus on potential is a developmental challenge that's most relevant when the pressure is on and the stakes are high. It's something that we can all learn to do more effectively. It takes courage to look closely at how you show up under pressure and to seek feedback on whether you more commonly see barriers or possibilities. It can help to practice the following:

- In moments when the pressure is the highest, state three positive outcomes that could occur because this negative thing is happening.

- Remind yourself that life is always a series of peaks and valleys. As a close friend of mine always reminds me, "life is defined more by seasons than by moments of failure or trouble."

- Resist the temptation to define only the destination or one measure of success. Think like an entrepreneur. As Saras Sarasvathy (2001) advises, think about who you are, who you know, what resources you have at your fingertips, and what you can do with this information.

We can change our mindset tendencies to see potential when others may only see a tree in the road.

SEEING WHAT COULD BE:

1. For every obstacle you're currently facing, what are three ways you can repurpose and rethink that obstacle to provide multiple positive possibilities?

2. In what ways are you engaging in "either-or" thinking instead of both "this and that" thinking?

3. What unsolicited voices or unexpected opportunities are presenting themselves to you that you might have missed?

CHAPTER 6 | ATTACKED OR OBJECTIVE: IT ISN'T PERSONAL

"Conflict is challenging because it involves at least two people who can move a conflict from a simple disagreement to a much deeper insecurity about our character."

Four years ago, I created the Leading under Pressure Inventory, which assesses people's strengths and challenges when under pressure. After speaking with thousands of leaders about the challenge of remaining composed, I began to generate the following working hypothesis about commonly list-ed areas of improvement. When leaders are in high conflict situations that involves other people, one of the most common struggles they experience is not taking things personally. In other words, the vast majority take conflict very personally and struggle to maintain objectivity when the pressure rises between them and others. And, it's not just leaders.

What is it that's happening inside of us when we're in an argument with someone at work or at home that causes us to take things so personally? It's oftentimes more than just losing our objectivity or that our sense of direction is being challenged. When someone disagrees with us or attempts to correct us, it challenges something deep inside us that is vulnerable or broken. Disagreement with others feels like a well-placed left hook that's directly targeting our identity.

Think about the last time that you asked your spouse or significant other whether or not they liked something. It could've been a pair of shoes, a painting for the wall, or your response to a disagreement you had with someone at work. If this loved one didn't immediately agree with you, it's likely that you took his or her reaction personally. It's funny because who would think that a pair of shoes could be connected to your identity! For many of us, here's what is happening in our minds. Level 1, you bought the shoes and you like the shoes. Level 2, you think that because your significant other doesn't like the shoes, he or she doesn't trust your fashion sense. Level 3, you globalize from shoes to thinking this is an attack on you. Level 4, your significant other doesn't trust you. Level 5, you're frustrated because you believe you should be perceived as trustworthy. Level 6, you know you're not always trustworthy. Level 7, you become insecure. As a result, what comes out of your mouth is, "You never like anything I do." But what you're thinking is, "You don't like who I am."

Trying to make a decision with someone else can quickly progress from trying to create mutual understanding to feeling like the situation is a direct personal attack on who you are and what you stand for. Why do we respond in that way? When people argue, it's often not just a disagreement. For many of us, it's a perceived disagreement about who we are and it brings awareness to our past mistakes.

The same thing happens at work. You receive an email from a co-worker that highlights the fact that you have a typo in an important document that's being sent to a customer. At the end of this email, it says, "We don't want to be perceived as unprofessional." You don't take this personally because it's a simple document with an error in it, you take it personally because what you hear them saying is, "You're unprofessional, and I don't trust what you're doing." Insecurity surfaces when your purpose and identity come into contact with your faults. Your co-worker may or may not feel this way. But, what could have been a simple correction to a document has become an attack on what you stand for.

Each of us has made mistakes, but our character doesn't end there. In order to trump this feeling that conflict with another person is an attack on our identity, we have to find a way to reframe the conversation that's going on inside of our heads. Three strategies to help reframe the conversation are to focus on the purpose for the relationship, identify our competencies and how to leverage them, and remind ourselves that although it's personal, it's not a personal attack.

WHY ARE YOU IN IT?

If you know a conversation that's likely to involve conflict is on the horizon, think intentionally about why you are there in the first place. Clarifying your purpose for being in the relationship can buffer what you might perceive is a personal attack on your identity. The relationship is more important than any pair of shoes you buy, or painting you hang.

SKILLS MATTER

In situations where we don't have the necessary strengths, we sometimes experience insecurity because there's an awareness that we're at the end of our competence. It's a feeling similar to that bad dream that many of us have had where we're told to play an instrument in front of 500 people, but don't even know how to hold the instrument. Or, we show up to school and there's a test that everyone except us knew about. When we're aware of the strengths, skills, and knowledge we do have, it's easier to maintain our objectivity and composure.

LIFE AND WORK ARE PERSONAL

I can't tell you how many times people have told me that they wished they didn't take things so personally. They wished they had the ability to remain objective, especially in situations when conflict and pressure are highest. The worst thing we can do is try to pretend that things aren't personal. The reality is that life and work are personal. High pressure moments that involve conflict with others are personal because they involve things that are important to us, but they're rarely attacks on our personal identity and character. It's not the fact that a situation is personal that's the problem; it's the challenge to our identity that gets in our way.

Conflict is challenging because it involves at least two people who can move a conflict from a simple disagreement to a much deeper insecurity about our character. Keep this in mind the next time you face a high pressure, high conflict situation with someone else. Being aware of it can help us maintain our objectivity.

Ninety-nine percent of the time, people's disagreements with us have little or nothing to do with our character. When the pressure feels highest, repeat the following in your head, "this feels like it is personal and about me, but it's not."

GAINING PERSPECTIVE:

1. Do you take things most personally when your character is challenged, when your competence is challenged, or when your purpose is challenged?

2. If you could take things less personally, what would be the impact on those around you?

3. Who in your life would benefit from you taking things less personally?

4. Of the three strategies (purpose, competence, it's not a personal attack), which do you think would be most helpful to you the next time you face a situation that challenges your ability to remain objective?

| CHAPTER 7 | THEIR SHOES OR YOUR SHOES: TAKING THE PERSPECTIVE OF OTHERS |

"Unless you are a psychic, we could all be a little better at listening to the perspective of others."

Few of us would argue with the fact that we could be better listeners. The problem isn't that we don't see the gap in our listening skills, but that there are many factors impacting our ability to listen well.[3] Short attention spans, our level of interest in what's being said, and our biases toward messages that reinforce what we already believe all impact our ability to listen. And, unless you are a psychic, we could all be a little better at listening to the perspective of others.

BEING IN THEIR SHOES

The ability to take the perspective of another person is often described as considering "what it's like to be in their shoes." Sometimes, the situation even calls for literally imagining what it's like

3. Sullivan, A. O (2011). The importance of effective listening skills: Implications for the workplace and dealing with difficult people. *Theses & Dissertations*, Paper 11

to be in the other's shoes. After nearly two decades of marriage, my wife and I still debate over where to park at a restaurant. Although I always think about a variety of factors that would impact how close we park, her perspective is oftentimes less complicated and is summed up in this question, "Do you know what it is like to walk in high-heeled shoes?" To which I respond, "No." The only time I have worn high-heeled shoes was for a Halloween costume 20 years ago. Some friends and I dressed up as the characters from the Robert Palmer "Addicted to Love" music video. As if finding a pair of size 12 pumps wasn't difficult enough, I recall the challenge and pain of trying to walk around the party. The reality is I don't know what it is like to spend many of my days wearing high-heeled shoes. I only begin to understand that moment when I actively imagine what it would be like to walk in shoes that look good, but have very little do with comfort. Most importantly, my first step should be to simply ask for my wife's perspective and then listen.

Putting yourself in the shoes of another person implies an ability to see the world from where the other stands. Although perception is still through our personal lens, this strategy pushes us to invest in understanding what the others see rather than focusing solely on what we see. If you've ever seen the movie Freaky Friday,[4] you'll know exactly what I mean. In the movie, a mother and daughter switch bodies and experience each other's lives for a day, but are still themselves. This teen movie demonstrates that although the experience is our own, we can have the ability to understand the other's perspective, thereby cultivating greater understanding.

What is it that causes us to make everything about us, and in turn, decreases our capacity to take on the perspective of oth-

4. Gun, A., (Producer), & Water, M (Director). (2003). *Freaky Friday* [Motion picture]. United States: Walt Disney Pictures & Gun Films.

ers? Pressure often triggers three different reactions in those of us who struggle to take the perspective of others. Cognitively (how we think), some of us experience a reduction in our ability to think ourselves into the shoes of someone else. Behaviorally, some of us experience an increase in the number of words that come out of our mouth in a minute. Emotionally, our feelings about ourselves and how we perceive people feeling about us can overwhelm our ability to see anything beyond three inches in front of our face. What we think, do, and feel can be our greatest inhibitors to seeing the perspective of others.

The irony of the cognitive, behavioral, and emotional responses to pressure is that they're often triggered by insecurity in our ability to see another's perspective, or because we think we're not being heard or understood. The problem is that people then tend to perceive us as uninterested in their perspective or as talking too much. The funny thing is that this can reduce their ability to see *our* perspective. And the vicious circle continues. We try to listen to them, they try to listen to us, and both of us feel like the other isn't listening. So what are we supposed to do?

Each of us has a self-serving bias and the first step is to be aware of that tendency within ourselves. We need to stop trying to be interesting and start being interested. If you're someone who fills many of the voids caused by pressure with talking, you probably don't even realize what percentage of conversations are filled by your voice. In this case, one of the first steps in developing your ability to see others' perspectives is to ask co-workers, family members, or close friends whether or not you tend to dominate conversations. Keep in mind that most of us underestimate how much time we actually spend speaking. Then practice shutting up and listening in.

Whether you struggle to think about the perspective of others, you talk too much, or your feelings get the best of you, we all could become better listeners with a little practice. This is best done by asking simple questions like, "Can you tell more about how you feel?" This question has to be followed by intentional silence that provides the person with a chance to communicate an honest answer. Being interested in another's perspective is about asking questions and working through the initial awkward stage of it being obvious that you're more focused on asking the right questions than purely being interested in their perspective. Like rusty water running through a faucet after you have been on vacation, allow yourself time to ask better and better questions.

The challenge is that sometimes when we're trying to listen, the concentrated look on our faces may be perceived as disdain or confusion. When I'm focused on listening, I have what my students call a "mean mug." The more I try to listen, the more I scowl. I feel no anger, contempt, or frustration. It's just the look on my face when I'm concentrating. Remind yourself that other people may misunderstand your attempt to listen more actively. Be aware that part of your role is to help others understand your intention.

GETTING THEIR PERSPECTIVE:

1. Is your ability to take the perspective of others most impacted by your emotions, your thinking, your actions, or a combination?

2. The next time you are in a high pressure conflict with someone else, the dare is to spend 30 minutes just asking questions.

CHAPTER 8 | VICTIM OR VOLITION: PERCEPTION OF CONTROL

"When we validate the power of our perspective we not only begin to see one way out, but oftentimes begin to see multiple paths out of a dark forest where everything looks the same."

Why is it that certain things feel like they happen to us, happen for us, or other things happen for no reason at all? Sometimes it's not the actual experiences that are most influential, but how we perceive them.

There are some experiences that produce such positive results that it's hard to deny the possibility that they happened for a reason. There are others you wouldn't wish on your worst enemy (or maybe you would - and that's a different book). A close friend of mine described his relationship with his mother as one where he was repeatedly told as a child that she wished he hadn't been born. Although he later reframed this as something that would help him relate to others with a similar experience, it's hard to imagine a world in which that message was ever a good thing.

EXPERIENCES THAT
HAPPEN TO US

Experiences that happen to us can range from making us feel a little bit out of control, to feeling like complete victims. At its worst, when we perceive experiences as only happening to us, we risk becoming serial victims. Serial victims label many things as happening to them, without a focus on things they can control. Although there are certainly things that happen to us over which we have little control, adopting this as our primary or only response can diminish our ability to see dozens of things we can change in an instant.

EXPERIENCES THAT
HAPPEN FOR US

Experiences that happen for us feel different. Whether the experience is positive or negative, we define them by the opportunity they provide. Conflicts at work may be reframed positively as creating more truthful conversations that allow us to make better decisions. An argument with a 13-year-old about whether he can have a phone sets the stage for more open communication in the future. It's not the outcome that makes the difference, but a difference in perspective. Viewing experiences as happening for us may help us to see the potential of a situation. However, at its worst, this perception may lead us to a view of life as only what it can give to us.

EXPERIENCES THAT
HAPPEN FOR NO REASON

A third way we may categorize challenging experiences is as having no purpose at all. We perceive these experiences as random emotional drive-bys that aren't targeting us, aren't intended to teach us anything, and could have happened to anybody. These are experiences that we perceived as "just happens" moments. They may connect to our purpose later, but in the moment, they simply passed by.

At their extremes, each of these ways of perceiving our experiences can be problematic and have implications for the people around us. If all we do is see what's happening to us, blame is our game. The short and long term problem with blaming everyone and everything is that it drains the energy out of us and everyone around us. For those who see everything as happening for them, continuous gain becomes the game and we risk being perceived as self-serving, narcissistic, and living in a world where life is about what it does for us. When we perceive most things as happening for no reason at all, our game is more defined by apathy. We deal with negative circumstances by communicating how little we care about them. We become like a six-year-old who starts to lose at Chutes and Ladders and explains, "I didn't want to play anyways." Although we project an attitude of not caring, everyone around knows that we care so much that our only strategy is to take our ball and go home.

CONTROL DOESN'T DISCRIMINATE

Before we beat ourselves up too much over our current perceptions of control, consider this: even those with the greatest power have the capacity to spend most of their time complaining about things they can't control. A while back, I had the opportunity to speak with one of the most powerful groups of leaders I could imagine. Their combined budget authority was in the multiple billions of dollars. I spoke to them about the power of a leader's perception of control and how pressure often causes us to see those things we can't change, as opposed to all the things that are within our reach to change. Ironically, I listened to this very powerful group of leaders complain about processes, systems, and people around them for two to three hours.

Although I was at a much younger point in my career, and somewhat intimidated by this group, I couldn't help but say to them, "I can't imagine being in a room with a more powerful group of people. You have more budget authority and decision-making power than any group of fifty people I could imagine. And yet, for the past few hours, I have listened to complaints about the five or six things that you cannot change, as opposed to the 1,000 things you could change tomorrow."

The interesting thing about our perceptions of control is that it transcends age, experience, and levels of influence. Our capacity to blame situations and people for what we're experiencing *does not* discriminate.

However, we want to be careful not to assume we can control everything. When we do, pressure between us and those around us may be the result. When terrible things happen we end up only blaming ourselves. However, if we spend all of our energy talking and thinking about things we can't control, we risk losing hope. Even Viktor Frankl,[5] who suffered unfathomable circumstances in a concentration camp, was able to identify something he could control in the midst of such an obvious lack of it. He said, "Even the helpless victim of a helpless situation, facing a situation he cannot change, facing a fate he cannot change, may rise above himself, may grow beyond himself, and by so doing change himself. He may turn a personal tragedy into a triumph."

---

5. Frankl, V. (1984). *Man's search for meaning.* New York, NY: Touchstone.

TAKING CONTROL

The positive message in all of this is that by simply identifying the things over which we have control, we can begin to change our perceptions. Think about one situation in your life right now that's causing pressure. On a scale from 1 (no control) to 10 (complete control), to what extent do you feel like you have control over the outcomes? The situations may cross the boundaries of your life and work, or your family and friends.

NOW, ASK YOURSELF
THESE QUESTIONS:

1. If you feel that you have some control (rating 6-10), what is one characteristic of that situation that makes you feel that control?

2. If you feel that you have little control (rating 1-5), what is one thing that you could do differently?

When problems trump our perspective, we lose our ability to see a way out. However, when we validate the power of our perspective, we not only begin to see a way out, but oftentimes begin to see multiple paths out of a dark forest where everything looks the same. Think about the last time that you or a loved one felt some kind of physical symptom that you couldn't explain (e.g., headache, backache, nausea). We can spin out of control trying to explain the mystery of our symptoms, or we can set an appointment with our doctor. Setting an appointment is taking control. You may not have all the answers, but this is a pathway forward.

The second step is to get clarity about how that first step is going to go. Although we can't always control the outcomes, we do have some control over the staging. In the business world, we call this contracting. Contracting isn't the same as a contract, but it has many similarities. A contract is a specific statement for how we expect people to think or behave in relationship to the decisions we're making. Oftentimes, we hesitate to clearly identify our expectations because we fear that people may think we're too controlling. The trick is to simply be clear about what's important to you and the intentions behind your actions. If I tell a student that going to college is going to be one of the most rewarding and challenging experiences of her life, it may have the potential to change the way she perceives her experience of college when it gets really tough.

TAKING BACK POSITIVE CONTROL

Although we all experience moments where we simply need to vent to a close friend or loved one about the things over which we feel no control, staying there can get us stuck in a helpless state. It not only gets us stuck, but it can also drain the energy out of everyone around us. If you struggle with this and would like to maintain your realism while getting focused on things within reach, the first step is simple. The start is to put aside your feelings of control just long enough to identify the important list of things you could change tomorrow or even in the next millisecond if you gave yourself permission to see them. This kind of control isn't about getting back at others (which is still a focus on what we can't control), but about finding those things that might improve the situation for everyone involved.

CHAPTER 9 | THE BALCONY OR THE PINHOLE: SEEING THE BIG PICTURE

"Pressure has the capacity to narrow our focus to the things that have very little possibility of helping us move forward."

For many Americans, soccer is boring. At the risk of infuriating the large part of Americans who love soccer, the reality is that many of us do not truly appreciate the game. The one thing most of us do appreciate is how cute kids are when they are first learning to play. I heard about how kids are like a swarm of bees, but it wasn't until my sons started to play that I really understood what it meant to watch a handful of kids chase the ball in a swarm around the field. When kids first start playing soccer, they tend to have an intense focus on the ball, but an inability to see the rest of the field or the other players.

In this past year, I coached my son's select soccer team. During one of the games, I pulled the boys together, pinned a ball to the ground, and told them all to look at the ball. I was frustrated because for 30 minutes of play, I watched them place 90% of their focus on the ball. I repeated, "Look at the ball because that's what all of you have been doing for the past 30 minutes." I then asked them, "What's happening around you right now?" One kid replied, "I don't know because I'm staring at the ball." Another boy responded, "I can't see my teammates." Then the lights started to go on.

When we stare at the ball, we miss the most important part of the picture. When we're on defense, we miss the fact that there is a wide open player from the other team who is in a position to score. On offense, we miss the fact that our own player is standing at the far post (the goalpost farthest from where you are positioned) just waiting for a pass. Similarly, when we're under pressure, we miss the many important things that are happening at the far post. As in soccer, most of the goals in life are scored on the far post. They're happening right behind us or around us, and not necessarily right in front of us.

As youth soccer players get older, they hear coaches use the phrase, "head on a swivel." Coaches teach kids how to simultaneously see the ball and see what is happening on the field around them. If your head is on a revolving swivel, you'll see the ball, the players around you, and the biggest opportunities of the game.

THE BALCONY OR THE PINHOLE

Pressure has the capacity to narrow our focus to the things that have very little possibility of helping us move forward. Whether it is boredom, resentment, anger, or fear that others might be mad at you, each of these feelings can cause us to focus our attention on the feelings and on the person triggering them. Doing so often causes us to miss the easiest pathways to composure.

I sat in a meeting a few days ago with a person who had been invited to speak to our team at work. Like any other meeting, we were all asked to provide a brief introduction to our guest. Instead of starting there, I asked our guest if he would introduce himself first. What I didn't realize was that he was going to spend the next hour and a half introducing himself. In my defense, I wasn't in charge of the meeting and I made several attempts to steer the conversation to the other people sitting at the table and to actionable items. I failed. I am fully aware that my impatience and need to control situations may have been a factor in this situation. In other words, I could have been getting in my own way and he could have been providing useful information that people needed to hear. Regardless of whether or not it was my problem or his, the fact is that there was a perspective to see. As soon as I took the opportunity to step onto the balcony above my own impatience and what I perceived as a lengthy and frustrating introduction, I saw that he had given me a gift. This guest described the multiple times he had been able to raise money for the different organizations where he served. I realized that if a person who doesn't have the social sense to stop talking could raise money and dreams, then maybe I could too.

I recognize that this next sentence may make me seem like a completely self-centered ogre, but he gave me the courage to believe in my own capacity to raise money. The moral of the story is not about fundraising, but about the fact that if we're willing to step onto the balcony above the fray, there are opportunities to take action or to see something that could change the trajectory of our careers or even our lives. It also allowed me to stop listening to the distracting voice in my own head and listen to what he was actually saying.

Pressure can cause us to look at a situation through a pinhole and miss all the opportunities around us. However, when we intentionally step onto the balcony and see the bigger picture, our eyes open to see lessons to be learned, people to come alongside, and opportunities to try something new.

A STRATEGIC STEP TO THE BALCONY

The challenge with seeing the bigger picture when we're under pressure is that pressure makes everything look smaller. We get laser-focused on our spouse who let us down, on a co-worker who once again didn't do their job, or on a person with hurt feelings. Seeing the bigger picture is a strategic response to pressure. As a professor of mine once said, "Being strategic is simply setting yourself up to take advantage of future opportunities."[6] In other words, seeing the bigger picture when we're under pressure is a strategic move that allows us to see opportunities that we would otherwise miss.

I once heard it said that human beings are the only species on earth that speeds up when lost. While I don't know if this is true or if we can test this, I do know that it makes sense. When we're lost and things are not as we wished they were, we can get hyper-focused on the one part of the situation where we feel pressure and consequently, miss everything else. Seeing the bigger picture helps us to remain composed when it is most difficult to do so. Seeing the bigger picture is about recognizing the larger systems of people and relationships around you. It is about considering the impact of our actions and our decisions on other people and reminding ourselves to keep our heads on swivels.

6. Herb Kierulff, Donald Snellman Professor of Entrepreneurship and Finance at Seattle Pacific University, personal communication.

SEEING THE BIG PICTURE:

1. What would be different for you if you had the ability to step onto the balcony when you are about to lose your composure? What would be different for the people who matter most to you?

2. Think about a high pressure situation you are currently facing. If you stepped onto the balcony above the fray, what would you see?

3. When you think about the people causing you the most pressure, what in their past or their present might explain the way that they are currently acting? The next time you are in a high pressure situation with another person, ask this person what is happening around him or her that is causing him or her to feel a certain way. This is a great question as it opens up the bigger picture for both you and this person.

CHAPTER 10 | **LIKE YOU MEAN IT OR JUST PLAIN MEAN: CONVICTION**

"A convicted person is someone who has the guts to communicate clearly about what matters to them and maintains an openness to the possibility that he or she could be wrong."

In the world of leaders, to show up with conviction is to show up like you mean it. When you show up like you mean it, it is obvious to everyone around you that whatever you are about to do or say is important and needs their attention. If there is one word that the hundreds of leaders with whom I have worked would use to sum up everything I taught them, I believe it would be the word "conviction." People follow conviction. Whether we like it or not, people follow people who are not only clear about where they are going, but also clear about who they are and what they want.

The Greek word for convict is "elencho," meaning to convince someone of the truth; to approve; to accuse, refute, or cross-examine a witness." Our convictions not only come from within us, but are continually refined through intense cross-examination. Our convictions are not shaped in the absence of others, but through inspiring moments and difficult conversations in which what matters most to us comes face to face with what matters most to someone else.

In order to show up like we mean it, something has to matter to us. Building convictions that have a deeper connection to a truth that is beyond ourselves requires an openness and a courage to come face to face with the possibility that what you believe is either untrue or may need further refining. It would be easier if this cross-examination only took place within ourselves. However, at its truest level, developing and communicating our convictions requires us to walk straight into the tension that what we believe is true and also in a constant state of refinement.

I am grateful to have an older brother who has served as one of my best friends and mentors. As a key voice in my life, he has helped me to understand that conviction means first listening to the needs of others around me, and then figuring out what is important to me, what I value, what I feel, and what I want to see happen. This lesson has impacted my ability to stay clear and true while never minimizing the experience of others.

I have a confession. I get frustrated by people who show up passively, especially those in whom I have made a conscious decision to invest my time in developing their leadership capacity. If you asked my students for a one word description of what I have tried to teach them, they would likely say "conviction". I have invested my career in developing leaders who are aware of their limitations and yet, in the face of them, show up like they mean it. I cannot tell you how many times I have asked this question of people - "What do you want and who knows?" It is not enough to know what is important to us, it is also important that others around us hear what is important to us. I believe so strongly in this because when I look at my students, I see the leaders who will lead me. I don't want to be led by leaders who are only about themselves, but by leaders who know what is important to them and are paying attention to what is important to others around them.

At a recent event in which I spoke to several hundred leaders, I noticed a woman in her early 60's sitting toward the back of the room. I noticed her because of the intense scowl on her face. She looked frustrated. I saw her elbow her way up the aisle and force her way to a seat in the front row. She still had that look on her face, but it had changed slightly. Her eyes were still evaluating me as the speaker, but her occasional nod told me that there was something that I was saying that was convicting her. I had stated that leaders who bring convictions that have not stood the test of cross-examination need to shut up. These are the leaders whose convictions are often separated from the needs of other people. During the following break, my scowling, nodding friend pulled me aside and convicted me. She said, "I need you to shut up and stop hesitating. I need the leadership development that you do. Your hesitation is getting in the way of what I need." The fundamental truth is this - people follow conviction. People follow leaders who show up with courage and clarity. People follow leaders who show up like they mean it.

A convicted person is someone who has the guts to communicate clearly about what matters to them and maintains an openness to the possibility that he or she could be wrong. The first step is to listen to what is happening in the lives of others around you and then show up speaking clarity about what is important to you. If you are open, the refining will happen naturally. You need only to show up like you mean it.

<u>WHAT MATTERS TO YOU?</u>

1. Write down the five most important things to you in your life and career. Why are these things important to you? What does this tell you about how you show up under pressure?

2. Consider a high pressure situation that is testing your ability to maintain your composure. What do you want to see happen? When will the other people involved hear your convictions?

3. Ask three people who are close to you if they think you should show up in your role with more conviction (like you mean it) or with less.

CHAPTER 11 | **WHO'S IN THE MIRROR: SELF-AWARENESS**

"When it comes to becoming self-aware, most of us aren't smart enough to figure it out on our own."

Have you ever gone into a restaurant bathroom, finished washing your hands, glanced up at the mirror to check for straggling hairs or soap on your face, and quickly thought, "I'm good." Most of the time, we are. We aren't missing anything that might embarrass or draw attention to us. Then it happens - that one in a hundred chance moment where we did miss something. You emerge from that bathroom with a passenger in the form of a piece of toilet paper attached to the bottom of your shoe. While you are thankful for the stranger or friend who whispers to you ten minutes later, "Hey, you have a piece of toilet paper dangling off your shoe," you're horrified as you think back through the last ten minutes.

Self-awareness isn't just what we see in the mirror. Self-awareness is completed by the people who encourage us and give us the tougher truths about things we don't see.

In my previous book, *Dying to Lead: Sacrificial Leadership in a Self-Centered World*, there is a chapter titled, "Who are you, really?" It is a chapter about self-awareness in which I define self-awareness as a combination of knowing ourselves, and at the same time, knowing how others see us. When I ask leaders whether they are self-aware, what I am really asking is if they understand who they are and how others see them. This is the double bind of becoming more self-aware. Self-awareness isn't as simple as yourself because it also involves an increasing understanding of how others see you.

Have you ever been in a situation where someone who knows you well provides you with feedback on how they think you could be a better version of yourself? In most cases, these feedback sessions come in the form of conversations with others at work or with close family members who have a complaint with how we have done something or how we have shown up in a certain situation. The fundamental starting point for these conversations is whether or not we are willing to hear someone else's perception of who we are, how we are performing, and then being willing to hold their perceptions in tension with our own. As I stated earlier, self-awareness always includes how we see ourselves and how others see us. Becoming self-aware is easier said than done, but some simple steps can helps us get started.

STEP 1: LOCATE YOURSELF ON THE MAP

When it comes to becoming self-aware, most of us aren't smart enough to figure it out on our own. This is where assessment tools can be key. Like looking at a map at the mall and trying to figure out where the statement "You are here" is on the map, good assessment tools are designed to tell you where you are right now. They may not necessarily tell you where to go next, but at least they will tell you where you are starting. Whether it's an assessment that provides you with feedback on your personality, your strengths or weaknesses, your calling or purpose, or your behavioral tendencies in certain situations, assessments like these can help us to become aware of certain things that we cannot see on our own. Although we should be cautious of over-interpreting of results, because we risk putting ourselves in boxes that don't completely capture who we are, assessments do provide insights that we may not see otherwise. The statement, "he's clearly an extravert," or "she is a dreamer" certainly miss the nuances of every one of our experiences, but these descriptions do help us move closer to a better understanding of ourselves. Like scaffolding on a building that helps us get access to parts of the building we otherwise couldn't reach, tools and assessments are there to help us understand parts of ourselves that we otherwise might not see.

STEP 2: PHONE A FRIEND

Receiving feedback from others or from some assessment about who we are, what we are doing well, and what we might need to change can be really difficult. Whether it's someone at work, a friend or family member, it can be difficult to hear. While challenging, these moments offer something else - the chance to test our currently working hypotheses. They are offering a chance to see whether or not our own views of ourselves match up with the views of others. Without that input, we are walking blindly into the pressure situations of our lives with only a half-baked reality about who we are and what we could change. But where do we begin?

The best way to start is to build what is often described as a board of personal advisors who will give you direct and honest feedback and who are invested in who you are becoming. They might be close friends or family members, colleagues at work, mentors or managers, but they are all invested in you and in being honest with you. Keep in mind that the intention in these conversations is to increase your self-awareness. Don't hesitate to make that clear to your board of advisors. We are one step away from increasing our self-awareness by asking one of these trusted individuals to join us for a cup of coffee.

STEP 3: PAY ATTENTION TO THE GAP

Self-awareness is not as simple as knowing ourselves and knowing how other people see us. Self-awareness is also a process of becoming a better version of ourselves. Tools and conversations that give us insight into who we are immediately highlight the gap between who we are now and who we could become.

Our primary challenge is not bridging the gap, but is in seeing ourselves in a constant process of discovery and movement forward. This is a process I describe as thoughtful action. The process of thoughtful action starts with self-awareness. This includes awareness, application, and action. Awareness is seeing something we didn't see before. Application is the impact of whatever we now see on ourselves and others around us. Action is what we are going to do about it.

Before we move to application and action, we have to reframe our journey into self-awareness. It's not about embracing a critic telling us how we should be better. Self-awareness is a process that both calls us out and sets us free into better versions of ourselves.

GETTING TO KNOW YOURSELF:

1. What are three things that you cannot help but do well? What are weaknesses that have gotten into your way? What are your top three character strengths?

2. Ask a friend to answer question one for you and then to meet you for coffee for one hour. Tell them your intention is to get honest feedback and become more self-aware.

3. Write a one page summary of who you are and who you are becoming. Now ask a friend to write a summary about you and meet them for one hour over coffee.

CHAPTER 12 | **BLAME OR GRACE: RECOGNIZING CONTRIBUTION**

"Grace calls out our mistakes, and washes them away."

Several years ago, a couple I was close with was going through a divorce. I ended up on the phone with the wife during one of the most difficult phases in their relationship. Although I should have kept my mouth shut, I cared about these friends and so, I offered her my hope. Rather than maintaining the power behind the blame I had heard, I wished that she and the husband would figure out what they each had contributed to their failing relationship. After pausing for a few seconds, she said, "I loved him too much." While that kind of response may have deeper insight that might illuminate recognition of loving him in her way and missing his needs, it didn't feel like that. Similar to the husband, her inability to intentionally question her contribution may have been one of the key factors in their eventual divorce.

If seeing potential or the bigger picture in a situation, understanding the perspective of others, or not taking things personally was challenging, the reality of recognizing our contribution to daily challenges is exponentially more difficult. This chapter is about our willingness to take responsibility for our contributions, both good and bad. Recognizing our contribution includes two steps: being willing to see the moments in which we have let others down, screwed things up, made mistakes, or even wronged someone else, and taking the full weight of the responsibility without offering half-hearted apologies or confessions peppered with a self-serving bias.

Taking responsibility is easy when we are talking about it over a cup of coffee where there is no pressure. Doing so becomes more difficult when the stakes are high and they involve other people who matter to us. The challenge with taking responsibility is that it is oftentimes in contradiction with the narrative that defines our western culture, in which our first response to failure tends to be blame.

I once heard Dr. Edward Friedman, a pulpit rabbi, therapist, and leadership development consultant, speak to a group of business leaders. One leader asked for the litmus test for identifying an individual with the greatest capacity to lead. Dr. Friedman paused and responded, "A person in any system of people who has the most capacity to lead is the person who can express him- or herself with the least amount of blame." He went on to describe that whether we are talking about our families or work relationships, these individuals are the people who constantly define themselves, sit clearly in who they are, and are willing to take responsibility in situations in which they have let people down. I would take Dr. Friedman's words one step further. The person who has the most capacity to lead well in high stakes situations is the person who not only expresses him- or herself with the least amount of blame, but is also willing to take full responsibility for what (s)he has done wrong.

It is important to note is that taking responsibility is not the same as blaming yourself, and it does not mean becoming a self-proclaimed martyr. Blame can quickly become a leadership catch phrase ("I'm going to take the blame for this one") depleted of action. Blame is a response that doesn't bring about the needed results. Blame ends the conversation and blocks a pathway out. Whether we are blaming ourselves or someone else, the product of blame is often shame. A good friend of mine often challenges me to, "Name the false narrative bouncing around in the back of your mind that promises to limit you today." He always goes on to encourage me by saying, "That thought paralyzes us, but it is a lie."[7] Shame is defined by pain, humiliation, or guilt, and oftentimes results in counterproductive loops that repeat in our thoughts. Grace, on the other hand, is defined by free and unmerited forgiveness and favor. What I am asking us to consider is that blame is shame-based while taking responsibility is grace-based.

It takes courage to recognize our contribution and the damage we have done to others. It may not be easy, but it is a leading act that requires a willingness to bear the weight of our responsibility. Taking responsibility is something less than natural. It is weird, upside down, and doesn't seem relevant in a society that is individualistic and focused on the preservation of self. In a culture that defines a person's value by strengths and accomplishments, it takes tremendous courage to shine light on something you'd rather not see. Shining this light includes at least two things. It includes what we need to change, but also the possibility that we can change. Some people would describe this as grace. As soon as we realize our need for grace, it highlights that from which

7. J. Morris, personal communication, January, 2016.

we need to be set free. Grace calls us to accountability, but also opens the door to forgiveness. Grace is something that sets us free. This is the profound thing about grace. Grace calls out our mistakes, and washes them away.

Recognizing our contribution and our need for grace, even in the most difficult situations, is built on our understanding that there is more to see. It is like staring at a door you are not certain you want to open. You know there is something behind that door to see, but you are afraid because behind that door lies truth. We want to live our lives in rooms full of doors that we open or shut at will and at times when it's comfortable to open them. We want to control seeing the reality of our contribution in our world. The most difficult doors to open are those that shed light on our shame, doubts, fears, or our mistakes.

Here is the powerful part. It is not only truth that lives behind those doors, but grace is there too. Grace is powerful because it not only brings the possibility of forgiveness where it may not be deserved, but it also is challenging because opening the door also brings us face to face with the reality that we need it - the reality that we have something that we might need to take responsibility for. When we take a look at our contribution to various relationships and situations in our lives, we are confronted by the truth of whether or not we have done the right thing, said the right thing, made a mistake, hurt someone else, or even hurt ourselves. The moment we consider opening one of those doors, asking for forgiveness, or getting real in relationships, is also the moment when we are confronted by our need for grace and the question of whether or not we deserve it. Our recognition of our need for grace both calls us to accountability and opens the door to forgiving ourselves and others.

Although grace and shame may sound like deep philosophical discussions, they impact us every day. Over the past year, I was coaching my sons' soccer team (they were on the same team – a bonus for a parent!), and I got frustrated when they boys on the team weren't working hard. After I asked them to hustle several time during drills, I saw a few kids walking slowly back to the huddle. If you've coached kids before and you value players who work hard, you know what I'm talking about. I gathered the team and asked, "Are you spoiled?" A couple of them giggled and said, "Yea, I'm spoiled." One of them asked, "What does spoiled mean?" I said, "Spoiled means ruined or rotten. You guys have heard the term spoiled brat. I want you to know that you are not spoiled because you are not ruined." I then asked them a second question. "Are you divas?" Again they giggled, and some of them said, "Yes." Others shook their heads no. When asked to define diva, they said it is someone who expects others to do things for them. I told them that sometimes they are divas. However, the difference between being a diva and being spoiled is that you can stop being a diva, you can stop expecting others to take responsibility for you, but you can't stop being ruined. In the same way, grace, unlike spoiled, reframes our mistakes and even offers us a clean slate. If we can build up the courage to open the doors where we hide our feelings about our failures and our successes, we open up the possibility of forgiveness and a fresh start for ourselves and others around us. Although shame is important because it calls us to accountability, letting it mark our identity without the possibility of forgiving ourselves and others is a trap that we can escape. It might be just one open door away.

While all of us could use a lot of grace, those of us who are leaders need as much or more than anyone. Whether you are a parent or a president, being the one who goes first requires you to take correction and accept forgiveness on a daily basis. You will screw it up, but you must keep going - not for yourself, but for the sake of those for whom you are responsible. The possibility that grace provides is less about an outcome and more about the courage we can muster to enter into real, vulnerable, and authentic conversations with others about our contributions, both good and bad. Whether or not others take the responsibility is not the point. Being more composed under pressure requires us to take the first step toward recognizing our contribution, even when we mess up.

OFFERING YOURSELF GRACE:

1. Think about a specific situation involving other people where you have failed to take full responsibility for your contribution, both good and bad. Take a moment to see what you have done right as well as the area where you may need to ask for someone's forgiveness.

2. Like every other strategy described in this book, recognizing our contribution is both deeply personal and deeply interpersonal. What are three doors that are difficult to open, but if opened, would provide forgiveness and reconciliation?

3. What is challenging about opening those doors? What are you afraid you might see?

4. What is the worst thing that could happen if you open one of those doors? Consider cracking open one and seeing what is behind it.

CHAPTER 13 | **THINKERS AND FEELERS: EMPATHY**

"Without emotional connective tissue, our world becomes run by the compulsions of individual leaders who lack the natural ability to take in new information, integrate feedback from others, and connect with the deeper emotional needs of those around them."

Would you describe yourself as an overly emotional person? Would you describe yourself as being in tune with what others are feeling? Have you taken a test that labeled you as a "feeler"? If you answered yes to any of these questions, you probably have a natural ability to understand and feel what other people feel. This is empathy.

According to Webster's Dictionary, empathy is defined as, "The feeling that you understand and share another person's experiences and emotions." You not only understand what others experience emotionally, but somehow, you feel what they feel. Webster's Dictionary doesn't separate understanding and feeling.

This connection between understanding and feeling is important because we have found that the ability to understand the perspective of another person is different than a person's ability to experience empathy. I'm not suggesting that we can't take another person's perspective and feel at the same time. However, they aren't the same thing, and it is perfectly normal to have one and not the other. Some have a natural ability to look at the world through the eyes of another person, but may not feel the emotions that flood through that person's veins. Conversely, others are empathic sponges who soak up the feelings and emotions of those around them, but do not necessarily have the ability to describe another's perspective.

THINKERS AND FEELERS

In our research on empathy we found that those who are high on empathy and those who are low on empathy show up very differently. Those lower on empathy also tend to be lower on taking things personally. Although we sometimes criticize those who don't feel as much as others, these are also the people who can stand in the middle of the storm and not feel like everything is a personal attack against them. They also tend to be higher on self-regulation. So not only do they not take things as personally, but they are better able to regulate their emotions in the moment. On the other hand, the people in our sample who scored higher on empathy also tend to score higher on taking the perspective of others and seeing the big picture. These individuals are the system connectors who can put themselves in others' shoes and more easily see the implications of their decisions. The challenge is that often these two types of people don't speak the same emotional language, and sometimes struggle to communicate with one another.

I have never been fond of the labels like, "thinkers" and "feelers." These labels are oversimplifications of the issues we face when it comes to understanding the perspective of others and empathy. Thinkers are feelers and feelers are thinkers. Thinkers experience emotion, but primarily feelings about their own situation. They generally don't internalize those same emotions when others are experiencing them. Likewise, feelers think. However, in times of high pressure, the emotions of others might trump their ability to think clearly. The challenge for the feelers in the world is that in our culture, being in touch with the emotions of others is often considered weak. Phrases and words like "touchy feely", "emotional", "needy" or "soft" are all too common. Thinkers, on the other hand, get a different set of labels. "Focused on facts", "clear headed", "results oriented", and "courageous" are some of those common words used to describe thinkers.

The problem with these labels is that although they capture pieces of reality, they miss out on the fact that we don't experience pressure in a vacuum. How we feel pressure is impacted by the responses of the people around us. Everyone brings their own perspective to high pressure moments. Only a naïve simpleton would assume that it takes one kind of person to make the world a better place. We experience the world together and we bring different strengths. The challenge is that we live in different realities that are defined differently because we think and feel differently.

When the pressure is on, it's not all fun and games for those who score lower on empathy. Unlike their feeling counterparts, it can be like walking into a dark room full of obstacles they can't see. These individuals often say: "I just don't feel what other people feel." It isn't until they bump into an obstacle that they realize there was something to see or pay attention to. Under pressure, they are sometimes perceived as disconnected or checked-out. However, these are also the people we oftentimes raise up as leaders because of our belief in their ability to think clearly, to set the direction, to stay objective, and to get results. It isn't surprising that "thinkers" oftentimes emerge as leaders, but it should be alarming because we might be missing the opportunity to raise up those who have a natural awareness and connection to the emotions of others.

For those higher on empathy, the challenge isn't bumping into emotions they can't see. For feelers, the challenge is to avoid the temptation to carry those emotions with them. In the presence of others experiencing intense emotional moments, they may have a tendency to become overwhelmed by the physical and emotional cues they perceive all around them. As if it wasn't challenging enough to feel what others feel, a strong tendency toward empathy usually includes the burden of managing the emotions of others, and that can be overwhelming. Those with empathy bring something to the table that has been mislabeled as a weakness, and is critical to building up leaders who have the whole package.

Composure isn't just about standing strong without emotion in the midst of pressure, but standing well in the midst of pressure. When it comes to empathy, those who have a lot of it need to understand that this is a strength. These are the individuals who naturally bring insight, mindfulness, and care to situations where others are missing these connections. All the messages you may receive that you are too touchy-feely or emotional are likely coming from people who don't understand that emotional strength in you. Empathy is too often labeled as a fault or a part that is broken and needs to be fixed. However, just because someone doesn't feel something as deeply as you do, doesn't make them any better at maintaining their composure under pressure. They just have a different set of strengths that allow them to show up well. Your natural ability to feel what others feel connects you to the experience, passions, joys, and sorrows of people in a way that others simply may miss. Some research has even indicated that those higher in empathy are perceived very differently from what we may expect. In a study of groups of people that work together, when rated by their peers, those higher in empathy were seen as having some key leadership attributes, such as their ability to relate to others and lead tasks.[8] Empathy has not only been mislabeled as weak, but also offers a strength we need in leaders.

CAN WE LEARN EMPATHY?

One of the most common questions I've been asked over the years related to empathy is whether or not it can be learned. Depending on how you define it, the jury is still out because it's just not clear and there is disagreement regarding it being something we can increase. Some of that disagreement is based on the varying definitions of empathy. As I said earlier, understanding the perspective of another person is different than feeling what that person is feeling. Just as important as whether or not it can be learned is whether or not you are willing to learn it. When we focus on whether or not it can be learned, we miss the power of our intentions and willingness to become a better version of ourselves. That motivation is connected to some deeper issues in each of us that include but are not limited to our willingness to sacrifice for others, to be vulnerable enough to feel what others feel, and to open the door to the possibility that what others are feeling about themselves is just as important as what we feel about them or about ourselves. As I've often said to the leaders I coach, what would it look like if you cared as much about what

8. Kellett, J. B., Humphrey, R. H., & Sleeth, R. G. (2006). Empathy and the emergence of task and relations leaders. *The Leadership Quarterly, 17*, 146-162.

others think of themselves as you care about what they think of you? While provocative, who among us couldn't benefit from that question once in awhile?

<u>UNLEASHING THE POWER OF EMPATHY</u>

The key to using your emotional strength under pressure is directly tied to something else in you. This is where other strategies discussed in this book can make all the difference. Who you are cannot be reduced to a list of independent strengths. Your capacity to be composed under pressure and fully leverage your empathy is directly related to your sense of purpose, your feelings of competence, and your identity. On its own, empathy can be a problem because it can cause some to focus most of their attention on attempting to manage the emotions of others at the expense of their own convictions and values. Because that's oftentimes a problem for feelers, getting clear about why you are in situations can be really important. If you know why you are in it and what matters to you, you are less likely to seek everyone's approval at the expense of your integrity. Knowing who you are and what you are about is just as important as feeling the pain of others. Empathy becomes a strength when we understand ourselves well, and get over the shame that may cause us to want everyone to be pleased with us.

As I discussed in the first chapter, one of the key pressure indicators for many of us is an awareness of when we start to feel something changing. Our own feelings of joy, anger, relief, and sadness, and our connection to those same feelings in others, are keys to us knowing when the pressure is on. People who have empathy have an extra gauge. You have a tool in your toolbox that other people sometimes may wish they had.

Imagine a world full of people who all lack the ability to feel what other people feel. Without emotional connective tissue, our world becomes run by the compulsions of individual leaders who lack the natural ability to take in new information, integrate feedback from others, and connect with the deeper emotional needs of those around them. This is not to say that those who are feelers don't have to be careful about being overwhelmed by emotion, but empathy is a key leadership strength. If you have it, the goal is to start using it, and not be ashamed of it.

CHALLENGES

1. For thinkers, avoid the temptation to think that those high on empathy are broken, overly emotional, or less competent. They are the keys to feeling what others feel. Without them, you are missing at least half of the picture of what is going on around you.

2. For feelers, embrace your empathy as a strength because it is not only what connects you to the emotions of others, but also gives them a sense that you care. This is a competence necessary to lead if we are to lead together.

FEELING BETTER:

1. When you feel overwhelmed by the emotions of others, what is it that allows you to hold onto yourself? For many people who are high on empathy, a clearly defined sense of purpose (why you are here in the first place) is really helpful.

2. What are the situations in which your ability to feel empathy has helped you or others move toward a better solution?

3. What other strategies from this book have helped you navigate the emotions of others, and to hold onto yourself when the pressure is on?

CHAPTER 14 | CHAOS OR CALM: SELF-REGULATION

"We don't achieve results on our own, we don't feel on our own, we don't define ourselves on our own, and we don't function best on our own. We perceive, feel, relate, and act in community."

In 2000, we set out to study the developmental journey of leaders in order to understand the moments that had a profound impact on the way they lead today. The question we asked was designed to help them share these powerful moments and the lessons that they learned. What we didn't expect was the intensity of how personal these moments were and how much pressure they caused. These key experiences weren't only about succeeding or failing at getting results, but were very personal stories about their ability to stand clear, calm, and collected in the middle of raging emotional storms.

Psychologists call this ability self-regulation. Therapists call this mindfulness or presence. People on the street call this maturity. Leaders often refer to it as composure. Self-regulation is the ability to monitor what we're thinking and feeling and to maintain our ability to make choices. Doing so allows us to manage our emotions and maintain our ability to see what is happening with others. It would be a lot easier if all of our problems were ones of execution – getting something done. However, the reality is that our ability to execute is directly impacted by how we show up under pressure and by our ability to see situations and people clearly. Self-regulation is a common issue for leaders because, by definition, they are responsible for not only managing themselves, but for managing the experience of others. At its core, self-regulation is about maintaining our ability to make a choice, and not acting out of compulsion. Those lowest on self-regulation struggle to act with intention, and are more often at the mercy of whatever they are feeling. Pressure causes it to get worse because we begin to respond to others based on our surging emotions, and not based on what's best in the situation. This doesn't mean you're a bad leader if you have a tough time avoiding the pressure to drop the hammer, or to light someone up with an email. It simply means that you might benefit from a little more self-regulation – an ability to take intentional and thoughtful action when others might simply react.

When we started to study self-regulation, we struggled with whether it was a strategy to help people become more composed under pressure, or whether it was actually a different way of describing what composure is all about. The reality is that it's both. There are ways to increase your ability to self-regulate under pressure. The good news is that the other strategies described in this book have an important role to play in your ability to manage your emotions in real time, especially for those of us who take things very personally.

Two of the primary contributors to your ability to regulate your emotions and continue to make a choice are a sense of purpose and seeing possibilities in the midst of difficult situations. More specifically, by being clear about why you are here in the first place and working hard at identifying possible solutions, you stand more effectively in the storms that life brings. Imagine yourself in an argument with your significant other. Those arguments often feel very personal and the people closest to us know how to push our buttons. While it may seem like a waste of time because you want to arrive at the answer, thinking about your purpose in that relationship and the potential that could come out of resolving those con-flicts well may have a profound impact on the outcome.

In many ways, self-regulation is what this book is all about. However, self-regulation is also something that some of us need to recognize we carry as a strength. If people have commented that you are calm under pressure or someone they like having around in situations of conflict, negotiations, or uncertainty, it's something you shouldn't dismiss. You might serve as the anchor that keeps people centered. You might even help them maintain their ability to regulate their own emotions. Also, realize that people who are good at holding themselves together under pressure can also be perceived as disconnected, impersonal, or lacking vulnerability. Because you are able to regulate your emotions, it may not feel necessary to communicate your feelings behind or intentions for your actions. I've watched this happen over and over again with teams that work together on a regular basis. Communicating the intention behind your actions may not only help them to understand you better, but in a strange way, may also help them remain more composed.

Our ability to manage our emotions, to remain composed, and to be the best versions of ourselves under pressure does not occur in a vacuum. In the soup of life, it is the mixture of our strengths and weaknesses that makes us all better versions of ourselves. Although that shouldn't be a revolutionary thought, many in our culture are driven by an "all about me" belief. The reality is that we don't achieve results on our own, we don't feel on our own, we don't define ourselves on our own, and we don't function best on our own. We perceive, feel, relate, and act in community.

BUILDING YOUR COMPOSURE:

1. What is something you are facing this week that is putting pressure on you? Recognizing that there probably isn't a perfect solution, what are the advantage and disadvantages of trying something different in that situation?

2. What is the smallest step you could take today that would have the greatest positive impact for you and for those you care about?

3. What about you allows you to stay centered when it feels like someone else is blaming you for a situation?

CHAPTER 15 | IT DOES MATTER!

> *"Our capacity to compose ourselves when the pressure is highest, to lead strong, and to lead with care into the most difficult situations of conflict and anxiety, may have the single greatest impact on our families, our teams, our organizations, and the world that surrounds us."*

Several years ago, I spoke to a group of student leaders at a university campus and tried to share as much wisdom as I could as they prepared for the next step of their journey. At the end of my talk, I told them I was going to read a quote from a philosopher who had thought deeply about life. I began with, "I've put my trust in you. Pushed as far as I can go. For all this, there's only one thing you should know." To my surprise, eight words into the song lyrics by Linkin Park,[9] the 300 students started to whisper those words with me. "But in the end, it doesn't even matter." It was a powerful moment for me. I didn't realize they would know who I was quoting so quickly, and even more powerful was that like me, they had memorized the words to a song that may have summed up a generation. When we finished the last line from that

---

9. (2001). In the end. [Recorded by Lincoln Park]. On *Hybrid Theory* [CD]. New Orleans, LA: Warner Bros.

song, I told them that there was one thing that those pop culture theologians may have missed. I said, "It does matter."

Since then I've realized that Lincoln Park may have had something right. Whether we like it or not, we oftentimes define our value and what matters most by our efforts and our ability to achieve the outcomes we desire. Think about how you define your own worth and effectiveness on a daily basis. Our self-worth is usually defined by the measures of success around us.

In our daily lives, we are surrounded by external pressures of success or failure that influence whether or not we believe we are worthy. Countless unread emails in your inbox, gadgets that measure the steps you take in a day, your job title, the number of promotions you achieve, or the size of your house. What does your achievement or failure to measure up to a perceived ideal of success do to your feeling of worth?

I am in no way suggesting that what we do and whether or not we measure our progress are not important. For some, a little more measurement and accountability would be a really good thing. What I am suggesting is that in the end, our effort and ability to make the mark is an incomplete definition of who we are. Our ability to compose ourselves under pressure is impacted by our results focus because it dismisses the power of perspective and self-worth. If we don't believe that we matter beyond our measures of external success, we risk becoming people who are reactive, full of blame, or buried in our own shame.

As we dug deeper into the data we collected on how people show up under pressure and the strategies they leverage to lead well when the stakes are high, we saw a very interesting pattern emerge. Not only were the strategies outlined in this book important, but our research also indicated that the strategies might be related to one big factor that was influencing people's composure under pressure. That factor is not about how much you achieve, but about how you see your world, seeing possibilities in the midst of barriers, and knowing why you are in a situation in the first place. The perspective that you adopt when you go into a high pressure situation may have more impact than whether or not you achieve your desired outcomes. For most of us, that is a revolutionary idea. It doesn't matter whether you are a parent, president, or pastor, how you show up is just as important as what you do.

I want to finish with a set of questions that might help you think differently, and therefore remain composed, the next time the pressure rises for you.

1. To what extent are you defining your character by over-simplified daily measures of your success?

2. What would change for you and for others if you could be more composed under pressure?

3. What are reasons, that have little to do with you, why people may be responding the way that they are?

4. If you could lighten the load of someone else with whom you are in contact, what could you do for them?

5. What are three things in this situation over which you have complete control?

6. What purpose could you serve that would make this situation better for as many people as possible?

7.   What would change if you spent less time caring about what other people feel about you and more time caring about what they feel about themselves?

8.   For what might you need forgiveness? Who may you need to ask for forgiveness?

As we get closer to answering these types of questions, it becomes less about our own need to feel better about ourselves, and more about developing those around us. Our capacity to compose ourselves when the pressure is highest, to lead strong, and to lead with care into the most difficult situations of conflict and anxiety, may have the single greatest impact on our families, our teams, our organizations, and the world that surrounds us. Life is full of high pressure moments that will challenge our capacity to be the best version of ourselves. The stakes are too high for us and for those we love to wait any longer. Let's get more composed when it matters most.

COMPOSURE COACHING TOOL

Think of a situation currently challenging your ability to maintain your composure. Considering each of the following, rating yourself high on 3 strategies, medium on 4 strategies, and low on 3 strategies. Have a conversation with a trusted other about their perceptions of you under pressure and whether or not their assessment of your strengths would be the same.

STRATEGIES	LOW	MED	HIGH	COACHING QUESTIONS
Sense of Purpose: You have identified a broader purpose and reason you are in this situation that is guiding your actions.				• What is the overarching purpose for your role in this situation that is bigger than the situation itself?
Perceptions of Control: You are able to focus on things over which you have more control, and less focus on things outside of your control.				• What are three things over which you have complete control in this situation?
Seeing the Big Picture: You recognize that the larger organization and system is often causing people to act the way they are and consider the impact of your actions on others.				• If you were to step onto the balcony above all the fray, what would you see?
Focusing on Potential not Problems: You see possibilities and potential instead of focusing on the problems, deficit and barriers.				• What purpose could the obstacles you see serve in opening up other possibilities for you and for others?

Taking Others' Perspective: You are able to put yourself in the shoes of others, even those who may be causing you the most anxiety.			• Assume that each of the stakeholders are acting the way they are for very good reasons. What is motivating them to make the decisions they are in this situation or to react the way they are?
Empathy: You feel what other people feel, sometimes even at the expense of your own values and convictions.			• How can you create the time and space necessary for other people to tell you what matters the most to them?
It Isn't Personal: You are able to remain objective and avoid the temptation to take things personally			• Assuming that other people aren't attacking or critiquing you, what might their intentions be?
Self-Awareness: You know yourself well and you know how other people see you.			• What are three things you know about yourself under pressure, and what can you put in place to ensure that you see yourself the way that other people see you?
Self-Regulation: You are able to compose yourself under pressure and to continue to make choices and not feel or act out of compulsion.			• What about you allows you to stay emotionally centered and composed when the pressure is on you?
Recognizing One's Contribution: You take responsibility for your contributions to situations and look at your own actions before looking for other people to blame when things don't go well.			• What is your contribution to the problems you are concerned with? • How can you be honest about your contribution (good and bad) to the situation?

Made in the USA
Monee, IL
10 October 2021